The Complete Guide to Wedding Etiquette

The Complete Guide to

Wedding Etiquette

by **Margot Lawrence**

Ward Lock, London

First published 1963
Reprinted 1971
Reprinted 1972
Reprinted 1974
Reprinted 1976
Revised and Reprinted 1979
Reprinted 1982
Reprinted 1984
Revised and Reprinted 1987
Reprinted 1987

ISBN 0 7063 6538-0

Published in Great Britain by
Ward Lock Limited, 8 Clifford Street,
London W1X 1RB,
an Egmont Company.

Phototypeset by MS Filmsetting Limited,
Frome, Somerset

Illustrations by Evadné Rowan

The publishers would like to thank *Brides and Setting Up Home* magazine for the financial information.

Printed and bound
by Casterman S.A.
Tournai, Belgium.

Contents

Illustrations

Introduction

Engagement and marriage are among the most momentous happenings in the lives of most of us: a time of rare joy, with a deep underlying significance, for upon the success and happiness of marriage, depends to a great extent the success and happiness of our whole lives. Perhaps it is the instinctive feeling of a turning-point in life which causes an upsurge of emotion in many of us at a wedding, whether we are personally involved or are just guests; emotion which often finds relief in a tear or two, paradoxical as this may seem upon a happy occasion.

Marriage has, furthermore, a wider meaning than the purely personal one, important as that is. So long as the family is the fundamental basis of civilised life, marriage has an important significance for society as a whole, symbolising the founding of a new family unit.

It is for these reasons that people of every race, colour and creed, instinctively seem to feel that a marriage should be surrounded by ceremony and formality. The host of customs, laws written and unwritten, traditions and usages that have grown up, may vary in detail, but all have the underlying purpose of expressing the importance of the occasion both to the man and woman concerned, and to society as a whole.

Yet it would be sad indeed if over-anxiety about "doing the right thing" and observing the correct usages of wedding etiquette, were to loom so large as to overshadow what should be a very happy time, or become the main preoccupation to the exclusion of human values.

For this reason the present writer and the publishers of this book trust that it may clear up all problems of procedure, large or small, of the kind that all too often crop up to puzzle or worry those who have the responsibility of organising a wedding; and that by providing them with a guide to any and every detail, it may leave them the more free to enjoy the actual occasion with untroubled minds, and add to the happiness of everyone concerned, making the wedding day a wonderful occasion long to be remembered.

1

The Engagement

Nowadays most young people require little guidance as to the formalities of courtship—indeed, such formalities hardly exist. An acquaintance develops into friendship, affection into love, and eventually the moment comes when they decide that they will get married. Families may help things along, discourage them, or be left in complete ignorance of what is in the wind, according to circumstances. Most young people take the view, and even their elders would probably agree, that courtship is entirely their own affair.

But the moment they make public their intention to marry, problems of etiquette and procedure begin to arise. The girl's friends will be asking to admire her ring; her father may want to know something about the young man's position and prospects. Aunt Edna will be asking if a notice is to be put in the newspaper because she must send a copy to those distant connections in Australia. The girl's mother will begin going misty-eyed over visions of her daughter in white lace (probably before even the girl herself has decided if she wants a white wedding or not!). Friends will write offering congratulations, and the letters must be answered.

Altogether, it is speedily borne upon both the

man and the girl that what they had thought was a purely private matter, affecting only themselves, is a subject of intense concern to everyone they know; and that if they are to avoid hurting the feelings of these well-wishers they will need considerable tact, patience, *savoir-faire* and kindness.

The first requirement of etiquette comes even before the engagement is formally announced, and that is, the customary interview between the father or guardian of the girl, and the young man she hopes to marry.

Formerly this was an occasion for asking the father's actual consent to the engagement, but modern couples know that they can, in fact, marry even without this consent, once they are of age. Nevertheless the usual procedure now is for the young man to ask for a personal interview with the girl's father; if he is dead, with her mother, uncle, or nearest responsible relative. At the interview, he should be prepared to state frankly his position and prospects; say enough to show that he has given some thought to how he can look after a wife and, later, a family; perhaps satisfy his prospective in-laws as to his own family background, education and general standing; and altogether show that he is a fit person to be entrusted with the girl as his wife.

In modern life, when young people travel freely around the world, it may happen that because of distance, a personal interview is out of the question. Then the best solution is for the man to write to the girl's father, setting out the kind of information listed in the previous paragraph and asking for her parents' approval for the marriage.

The girl should write at the same time saying how happy she is and how she feels sure that her parents will like the young man when they are able to meet him.

If the parent is satisfied as to the man's character and position and gives his consent, all is well; but even if consent is refused, the couple are still at liberty to announce their engagement. The consent of both parents is normally necessary for the marriage of anyone under 18 at the time of the ceremony. If consent seems to be unreasonably withheld, it is possible to make an appeal to the courts for permission to marry, but this usually results in a lot of ill-feeling and embarrassing publicity, and it is usually wiser to be prepared to wait.

In the case of a very young marriage, it should perhaps be mentioned that a couple cannot in any circumstances be legally married if either or both are under the age of 16.

If a couple, both over 18, decide to marry without consent, it is kinder and wiser to let their parents know the time and place of the wedding, to give them the opportunity to attend should they change their minds. It is better, too, for young people to refuse to give a promise not to marry, than to give their word and then break it.

In the vast majority of cases, however, parents are happy to give their consent to the betrothal, and the next problem of etiquette is: Announcing the Engagement.

This is always done by the girl's family. It can be done in three ways: by a newspaper announcement; individually to friends either in person or by letter; or at an engagement party. Most people use all three methods—press announcement and letters for more distant friends, and a party, large or quite small for close friends and relatives who can conveniently come.

If there is to be a party or personal announcement, these should be timed so that the press announcement, if any, comes after close relations and friends have been told. They should not be left to learn of the engagement from the newspaper. All letters announcing the engagement should be posted to arrive at the same time.

The usual form for a press announcement is as follows:

> Mr. A. E. Brookman and Miss R. A. Walters
> The engagement is announced between Alan Everett, elder son of Mr. and Mrs. S. Brookman of 18, Pont Square, Westminster, and Rosemary Anne, only daughter of Mr. and Mrs. J. Walters of Oak Cottage, Bramfield, Gloucester.

There are some permissible variations upon the above form. For instance, if the fiancé is an officer, his decorations, rank and branch of the Service are usually given in the announcement itself, and this necessitates including his surname: e.g., "The engagement is announced between Captain Alan Everett Brookman, D.S.O., The Rifle Brigade, elder son of . . ." etc.

Where the parents of either the man or the girl are divorced, or where one of them is dead, it is usual to make this plain in the wording of the announcement, which would be along these lines:

The engagement is announced between Alan

Everett, elder son of Mr. S. Brookman of 17 Pont Square, Westminster and of Mrs. R. McCarthy of 717 Sackville Street, Dublin, and Rosemary Anne, only daughter of the late Mr. J. Walters and of Mrs. Walters of Oak Cottage, Bramfield, Gloucester.

The name of the bride's mother *must* appear in the announcement, even if she is divorced and re-married. To omit it is only possible if there has been some kind of open scandal about her.

If the bride's mother has really moved out of her life, and cannot possibly be associated with the announcement, the wording might then be as follows "... and Rosemary Anne, daughter of Mr. J. Walters and step-daughter of Mrs. Walters of Oak Cottage ..." etc. But it is best, from the point of view of etiquette and appearances, if the bride's mother can be associated with the wedding of her daughter; and many families prefer to "bury the hatchet" for this occasion rather than allow unpleasantness and recriminations to spoil a happy time.

If the bride is a widow, the usual form for announcement is:

Mr. A. E. Brookman and Mrs. J. Jeffreys

The engagement is announced between Alan Everett, son of Mr. and Mrs. S. Brookman of 18 Pont Square, Westminster, and Rosemary Anne, only daughter of the late Mr. J. Walters and Mrs. Walters, of Oak Cottage, Bramfield, Gloucester, and widow of Dr. John Jeffreys of Chester.

The last eight words can be omitted, the reader assuming that she is a widow simply because of the difference in her surname and that of her parents. A similar form might be used, omitting the last eight words and using her own initials (Mrs R. A. Jeffreys) if she has been divorced.

If the engagement is expected to be a short one, the announcement usually begins with the words "The engagement is announced and the marriage will shortly take place between . . ." and then goes on with the names and other details as above; or it may be worded "A marriage has been arranged and will take place on November 7, between . . . etc."

Announcements as given above are suitable for the "Forthcoming Marriages" columns of the leading national newspapers. If it is desired to announce the engagement in the local press, copies of the paper in question should be studied for permissible variations in the style of wording; if in doubt, the above examples are always correct.

If the bride and/or groom are well known locally, so that their engagement would be of interest as a news-item (as distinct from a paid-for announcement), it is quite in order for an announcement to be sent to local papers likely to be interested, for insertion as a news paragraph. Then the wording would be as follows:

"Mr. and Mrs. J. Walters of Oak Cottage, Bramfield, announce the engagement of their daughter Rosemary to Mr. Alan Everett Brookman, son of Mr. and Mrs. S. Brookman of Pont Square, Westminster. The wedding will take place in the spring."

"Miss Rosemary Walters, whose family has lived at Oak Cottage for over 20 years, was educated at St. Mary's School, Bramfield and at London University and for the past year has been working in the almoner's department at Bramfield Cottage Hospital.

Mr. Alan Brookman, who was educated at St. Paul's School and served in the Royal Navy, is resident surgical officer at Gloucester Hospital. While at Cambridge he played full-back for the university."

An announcement of this kind should confine itself to strictly factual details about the education, careers and serious spare-time interests of the young people. Anything gossipy or savouring of publicity-seeking should be avoided, though it is permissible to supply further information and/or photographs in response to a request from the newspaper.

THE ENGAGEMENT PARTY. This is given by the parents of the girl, and is usually quite a small intimate affair, limited to relations and close friends. It can be a dinner, cocktail party, luncheon party or anything else that seems convenient. There is little special etiquette involved. The engagement is announced and the health of the couple is proposed in a quite short speech, usually by the girl's father, though an old friend or favourite uncle may be asked to do it instead. The young man replies to the toast, thanks everyone for their good wishes, concluding by proposing the health of the girl's parents, and his own if they are present. No other toasts or speeches are necessary.

Sometimes it is more convenient to announce the engagement to friends by letter and through the press and then to hold a small celebration party a few days later, but this is a matter for personal choice. Occasionally, if there is a big dance or party already planned, it may be decided to make a formal announcement of the engagement then.

THE ENGAGEMENT RING. The custom of the young man giving his fiancée a ring in token of their contract is very old. The only formality which is still strictly observed is that the ring is not worn publicly until the engagement has been announced, after which it is worn on the third finger of the left hand.

There is no rule as to the type of ring used, either for the engagement or for the wedding ring itself. Sometimes the young man presents his fiancée with a family or heirloom ring. Most often a ring is bought for the occasion and then the bride customarily chooses the style she prefers. It need not be new, however; antique rings are often favoured and many couples prefer to buy one of these.

Other couples, again, may decide to dispense with an engagement ring, especially if the engagement is to be of short duration; they may prefer to save the money towards their future home.

The ring is usually presented as soon as possible after the engagement is agreed. If there is an engagement party, it may be publicly given then.

Alternatively, the man may produce the ring as soon as he receives a favourable reply to his proposal; though most brides would prefer the chance of choosing the ring themselves.

This choosing of a ring can be an occasion calling for tact, because inevitably the unromantic question of cost enters in. The best plan is for the man to visit the jeweller beforehand and arrange for a selection of suitably priced rings to be produced when he returns later with the girl. Then she can choose what she prefers without fear that she is over-straining his budget.

Men do not normally wear engagement rings. If the girl wishes to make her fiancé an engagement present, a cigarette lighter, a decanter or pair of cuff links are suitable gifts.

GIFTS FOR THE FIANCÉE. It is not usual for a couple to exchange presents during the engagement unless on some special occasion such as a birthday. Normally, an engaged couple are saving towards their home and lavish presents would be out of place.

FAMILY ETIQUETTE. If the two families are well known to one another, the new relationship will not mean a great change in the situation. Then, the correct thing would be for the man's mother to invite the girl's family to a small informal family dinner party; if circumstances make a luncheon party seem more appropriate, that would be quite in order, or, if the distance is too far to travel for a single meal, the man's mother might invite the girl's people to spend the day; it all depends upon circumstances.

Engagement presents

The main point is that it is for the man's family to make the first move. If the two families are not well acquainted, the parents of the groom should call on the girl's parents as soon as possible after the engagement is announced. If his parents are no longer living, the visit should be made by the head of his family or some similar responsible relative. It should be returned by the girl and her mother, or father, within three days.

If the families live at so great a distance as to make a meeting impossible, then the man's mother should at least write a pleasant letter to her prospective daughter-in-law, if they have not already met, saying that she is happy at the engagement and hopes for a personal meeting soon. It is quite in order though not absolutely obligatory, for her to write in similar vein to the girl's mother.

ENGAGEMENT PRESENTS FROM FRIENDS. It is unnecessary for friends to give presents to the engaged couple, though if they wish to do so, there is nothing against it. The most usual thing is to give the girl some quite small present towards her future home—a table cloth, cushion cover, pair of guest towels, etc., is usual from friends, or an aunt might give a small bit of family silver or piece of family jewellery, to mark the occasion.

THE "SHOWER" PARTY. An American custom which is occasionally adopted in Great Britain is for young women friends of the engaged girl to give a "shower" party for her. This traditionally takes the form of a tea party at which each guest brings some small gift towards the bride's new home. Thus at a "kitchen shower" gifts might include tea towels, dusters, egg whisk, a saucepan, and similar items of equipment; other types of shower might be a garden shower with gifts of seed packets, plants, and garden implements, or a linen shower, when small gifts of household linen are contributed by the guests.

This is a pleasant custom to adopt when, say, the bride is going some distance away to be married so that her friends could not all be present at the wedding; it gives them an opportunity to celebrate and congratulate her. On the whole, however, the alternative convention of the larger joint present to which all the girls in the office, club, or other organisation, have the chance to subscribe, is still more popular.

THE LONG ENGAGEMENT. Now that the majority of girls continue in paid work after their marriage, there is usually no financial reason to make a long engagement necessary, and the question of a long engagement usually only arises if the man is completing a period of professional training, if he has to be abroad for some time, or if the couple are extremely young and it is thought best to wait a while before marrying.

Since long engagements are now the exception, most young people in this position prefer to have an unofficial engagement, made known only to close friends and relatives, and to make a public announcement only when the wedding date is within a matter of months. The man may give the girl a ring, but she does not usually wear it publicly until the engagement is formally announced.

BEHAVIOUR OF THE ENGAGED COUPLE. Engaged people should be wary of adopting a too-proprietory air towards one another in public or of showing demonstrations of affection that may embarrass others. At the same time they must each make the happiness and welfare of the other their first consideration.

It is not in good taste for an engaged girl or man to be seen regularly in the sole company of another member of the opposite sex. It is however quite acceptable for him or her to go to parties alone or to go out with a group of friends in the evening if the other partner is unable to be there. Naturally any invitation should include both man and girl.

THE BROKEN ENGAGEMENT. This is an embarrassing ordeal for both parties, but better that than a disastrous marriage.

If the engagement has been publicly announced in the press, it is usual for the girl's family to insert a very brief announcement in the same newspaper, as follows:

> The marriage arranged between Alan Everett Brookman and Rosemary Anne Walters will not now take place.

When announcing a broken engagement it is unnecessary to give full details of the couple's parentage and addresses, as the announcement is presumably only of interest to readers who know them already.

When an engagement is broken, the girl should

return her engagement ring to the man, and also any presents of value which he may have given her. Depending upon the circumstances in which the engagement was broken, it sometimes happens that the man says she may keep the ring, or other gifts and if so, there is nothing against doing so; in this case she would transfer the ring to her right hand and wear it there.

The disposal of letters sometimes presents a problem. To return them may seem an unnecessarily dramatic gesture, but to retain them is usually unwise unless actual legal questions are likely to arise. Probably the most commonsense course is simply to burn them.

Whether or not it is she who really wishes to end the engagement, the responsibility for breaking an engagement should be left to the girl, since it is usually she who bears the brunt of any gossip which ensues. Outsiders should be left to assume that it was entirely her wish that things were broken off, even if it is in fact the man whose ardour has cooled.

The girl or her mother should inform close friends and relations by letter:

> "Dear Jane, Since I last wrote to you, Norman and I have decided to end our engagement. We both felt that it was the right thing to do. Yours affectionately, Jennifer".

No other explanation need be offered, nor should it be sought by friends. A brief and sympathetic acknowledgement is all that is called for:

> "My dear Jennifer, I was so sorry to hear the news of your broken engagement, as however

wise one may feel such a course to be, it cannot happen without some heart-searching. I sincerely trust that time will heal the hurt and feel sure that it will prove to have been for the best in the long run. Yours sincerely, Jane."

If the engagement is broken after the wedding invitations have been sent out, the mother of the bride will need to cancel these. It may be necessary to send a letter or telegram or to telephone, but if time allows, a card engraved in the same style as the actual invitations is usually sent. It should be worded as follows:

Mr. and Mrs. John Walters announce that the marriage of their daughter Rosemary Anne to Mr. Alan Everett Brookman will not now take place.

As soon as possible after this announcement, the couple should return to the donors, with a brief courteous letter, any wedding presents which they may have already received.

2

What kind of Wedding?

It is important to plan the wedding well ahead, especially if an elaborate ceremony is wanted, followed by a big reception for a large number of guests. Fashionable churches and leading restaurants and caterers are often booked up months ahead, especially if the wedding is planned for a Saturday during the popular spring or summer months. Invitations take time to engrave or print; there are the dresses to be planned and made. And the happy couple have, in addition, the often difficult and always complicated task of finding and furnishing their new home.

The questions to be decided at the initial stage of planning are:

1. Where and when will the marriage be solemnised—in a church or other place of worship or at a register office? At what time, day, month?
2. Will there be a reception, and if so, where will it be held? At the bride's home, at the house of a friend or relation, or in a hotel, restaurant, or hired hall?
3. Will the reception be a large and elaborate affair, or something simpler? How many guests should be invited?
4. Will the bride have any attendants and if so how many and who shall they be? Are there to

be ushers, and if so, who? What about a Guard of Honour? The bridegroom will need to think about who is to be his best man.

5. What will the bride and her attendants wear? This is important because it largely sets the keynote for the whole wedding party.

There are a large number of decisions on matters of detail also—flowers for the church and wedding party and the question of music and bells at the church, for example, but these details can be left till a little later.

Traditionally, the final say on all these various points rests with the bride; it is "her day" and everyone will want her to be happy. At the same time, she should consider other people's feelings and convenience—not to choose a day which may conflict with previous important business obligations of her fiancé or father; not to ask for a bigger reception than the family can reasonably afford to give her, and so on. The bride, her family and her fiancé may decide the various points together, or they may call the bridegroom's family into consultation, discussing everything at an informal dinner party.

The date of the wedding can be influenced by the date from which it is convenient for either partner to take their holidays from work. Or, if either is changing jobs and taking a long break before starting a new one, it may be a good idea to arrange things so he or she has some spare time, perhaps before the wedding, to prepare the new home—organise furniture removals, supervise renovations, plumbing, telephone connecting and so on.

Another point to consider, with regard to the

honeymoon, is that out-of-season air travel and package holidays can be much less expensive than those taken in the peak holiday season.

It is always wise to organise travel and hotel accommodation well in advance, as these can become fully booked many months ahead, especially in the summer months. Scheduled flights are usually cheaper if booked some time ahead too.

A frequent misunderstanding concerns the place of the wedding. Many couples prefer a simple, unostentatious wedding, with the bride wearing a day outfit rather than the traditional gown and veil; they may feel that a "big" wedding is an unnecessary expense, or there may be family mourning, or they may genuinely prefer simplicity rather than show. Unfortunately the traditional church wedding has become so linked with all the paraphernalia of bridal clothes, attendants, flowers and so forth, that many people do not realise that a simple quiet church wedding is equally possible, with just the families and close friends present, everyone wearing ordinary clothes and the emphasis placed firmly where it should always be by rights, on the religious aspect of the marriage and mutual exchange of vows, rather than on outward display. It is always a pity for anyone who would like the church's blessing on their marriage, to forego this privilege in favour of a register office wedding, just because one has come to be equated with "simplicity", the other with "show."

But this, as everything else connected with the wedding, is for the bride to decide.

If she opts in favour of a religious ceremony, the time, date and place should be confirmed with the clergyman concerned, before arrangements are made for printing of the invitations. Similarly, the caterers or hotel for the reception will have to be consulted before this detail can be taken as settled. The bride's mother makes arrangements with the caterers, florists and printers; the bridegroom makes arrangements either with the clergyman or registrar who will perform the ceremony. In practice the young couple usually go along by appointment to see the clergyman and discuss arrangements with him. If they wish to have special music at the ceremony, bells rung, or special floral decorations, the matter should be mentioned at this initial interview.

TIME FOR THE WEDDING. Weddings may take place at any time in the year, though Lent is considered less suitable than other times, and Jews may not be married on the Sabbath (sunset Friday to sunset Saturday) nor on festivals and certain other specified days. Register office weddings do not take place on Sundays nor public holidays.

The time of the day is largely a matter of personal convenience. If guests have to come from far, it should not be too early, yet it must allow time for the newly-married couple to get away by whatever train or air flight they are planning for the start of the honeymoon. Hence, midday or early afternoon are the most popular times. The wedding may, however, legally take place in a church, chapel or registrar's office at any time between 8 a.m. and 6 p.m. Jewish marriages may take place at any hour of the day, as may marriages by Special Licence.

In fixing the time of the wedding it should be borne in mind that a morning wedding often implies a full-scale wedding breakfast for the reception; for an afternoon wedding a less elaborate buffet tea is usually arranged.

Weddings in Great Britain may not take place in the open air, nor in private houses, except for Jewish weddings, or in the very rare cases where such houses are registered as places of religious worship (as has occasionally happened with Quakers who have regularly held their meetings for worship in a private house.)

INTERVIEW WITH THE CLERGYMAN. Besides settling the date and time for the wedding, the clergyman will ask a couple who are to marry in the Church of England, whether they wish to marry according to the 1662 ceremony in which the bride promises to "obey" and the husband to "endow" her with all his worldly goods; or the 1966 Series 1 ceremony which provides the option to omit the word "obey" and in which the husband promises to "share" his goods; or the 1977 Series 3 ceremony in which the emphasis is on sharing. If in doubt, it is worthwhile to read through the three possible services beforehand.

The clergyman may also ask if the couple would like a sermon at their wedding—a short discourse on the duties and responsibilities of marriage. If they do not wish for this, they can reply that they feel the Prayer Book words in themselves supply all that is needed.

The clergyman will also be able to advise the bridegroom of the scale of fees at the church.

Interview with clergyman

Any parishioner is entitled to be married at his or her own parish church (even if it be St. Margaret's, Westminster); but if one wants to be married at a "fashionable" church where one is not a parishioner, then one may incur considerable extra expense. There will also be fees for the use of the organ, the organist and choir, if music is wanted, and for the bellringers if they are asked for.

The bride and bridegroom may choose the music for the organ and choir in consultation with the incumbent, or the choice may be left to the organist, see pages 102 and 103 for full details.

The clergyman will also advise on the fees payable to himself, the clerk and the Parochial Church Council. Where there is no clerk, the clerk's fee is payable to the person performing the duty. At Jewish weddings the fees can be discussed with the secretary of the synagogue, and the priest's present is usually sent to him by post.

It sometimes happens that the couple would like to have the ceremony performed not by the parish priest but by a friend or relation who is a priest. There is not usually any difficulty about arranging this, but the parish priest's permission must first be sought.

It is important that the fee still goes to the parish priest, not to the visiting man. Sometimes it is possible to arrange that the friend from outside conducts one part of the ceremony, the parish priest another, where both are friends of the family.

A similar position arises with organists. If one happens to know someone who could play for the wedding, the regular organist at the church must still get the fee and must be tactfully consulted before another person is brought in to play.

Both organists and clergymen usually waive their fees when professional colleagues are concerned. For instance, if a choir member were being married, the rest of the choir and the organist would usually turn up to provide music as a courtesy and without fee.

Bell-ringers are usually only too glad of an excuse to indulge their passion for ringing, so if the church has a good set of bells it is not difficult to arrange that they be rung for the wedding; but here again there will be a small fee per rope. This, again, is something that should be discussed at the initial interview with the clergyman. If a day is chosen which is a busy one for weddings at the church, it may not be possible to have the bells rung both before and after the ceremony.

DOUBLE WEDDINGS. It sometimes happens that two girls (or, occasionally, two brothers) would like to have a double wedding. This, again, should be discussed with the clergyman at the initial interview. There is certainly this to be said in favour of the double wedding, that it does allow of doing things on a more lavish scale, with a more elaborate reception, church decorations, and so forth, than might be possible if the available money had to be spread over two separate weddings.

The usual procedure for a double wedding, if the girls are sisters, is that the elder arrives at the church and walks up the aisle upon the arm of her father, the younger escorted by a brother or some other male relative; but the father "gives away" both girls. They usually have one set of bridesmaids between them. The service proceeds quite straightforwardly to the point where the couples have to exchange their vows and be pronounced man and wife; one couple is taken first through this part of the ceremony and they then stand aside while the second couple make their promises. After this the service again continues in the ordinary way as for a single couple.

When the marriage register comes to be signed, the couple who took their vows first sign it first, with their witnesses, and the other couples, with their witnesses, follow after. In the processions up the aisle before the ceremony, and down through the church again afterwards, the bride who takes the vows first will walk first, the other girl second. In deciding which of them should take precedence in this way, it is usually the older girl who is accorded precedence. Similar precedence applies to the families: i.e. the family of the groom of the older girl sit in the first pew and take precedence at the reception, the "in laws" of the younger bride take second place. Needless to say, this precedence is a purely formal thing, because somebody has to go first; it does not imply that the second girl and her in-laws are any less important; often it can be arranged that one girl takes precedence on arrival at the church, the other in the procession after the wedding.

WEDDING OF A WIDOW. If a woman is quite a young widow, her wedding may follow more or less upon the arrangements outlined throughout this book as for a single girl; except, of course, that it is inappropriate for a widow to wear the traditional white gown and veil. Apart from this one difference her clothes may be as elaborate as she pleases, and the ceremony can be just as beautiful and the reception as large, as for a first marriage. Inevitably, however, it will lack something of the spontaneous atmosphere of joy of her first wedding, and some brides may feel they would prefer a smaller, quieter, ceremony and reception. It is entirely a matter of taste.

Older widows usually have a quiet and simple ceremony followed by quite a small reception.

In the case of a girl marrying a widower, she is quite entitled to have the full wedding pomp and finery, if she wishes. The fact that the bridegroom has been married before does not affect the case.

MARRIAGE OF DIVORCED PEOPLE. If either party has been married before, and has a partner still living, they cannot expect or demand to be married in church, though it does sometimes happen that a clergyman can be found who is prepared to perform the ceremony in his own church.

A better solution, if the couple genuinely want the church's blessing upon their union and know a clergyman in sympathy with them, is to be married first at a register office and then to go at once with their immediate relations and close friends, to the church, for a small unofficial service of dedication and blessing.

If the couple have many friends, it is quite in

order for them to have a fairly large reception following a register office wedding, though the reception is not usually such a formal affair as that following a full-scale church wedding. If they prefer, they can dispense with a reception altogether, or invite just a few friends to a luncheon or cocktail party or whatever is convenient.

WHEN TIME IS SHORT. It occasionally happens that a wedding has to be arranged at rather short notice, usually because the bridegroom is being sent abroad with one of the Services or for his firm, or, in these days, because the young couple has the chance of getting a house or flat that they would lose if they delayed.

When this is so, it is often hard to arrange a big reception, plan wedding clothes, and so forth, in the time available. At the same time one wants to avoid giving the impression that there has been any deliberate wish to exclude friends. It is usually best to do things in very simple style (hand-written invitations, a simple cocktail-party type of reception, and so on) and to include as many friends as possible, rather than attempt to plan an elaborate function but invite only a few people.

PLANNING THE RECEPTION. The bride's parents give the wedding reception, are the hosts at it, send the invitations and, most important of all, pay for it. No responsibility is undertaken by the bridegroom's family. The only exception to this would be, if the bride's family lived overseas or were dead, and she had no relations available who could act in their place; in this case the bridegroom's family might give the reception for her. The impression to be avoided is that anybody might think the bride did not want her own family around on this very important day.

The main thing to decide, at the initial planning conference, is what size of reception will be best. Most of the other plans will depend upon the number of guests to be invited; and however simple and unelaborate the style of the reception, its cost will largely depend upon the number present rather than upon the lavishness of the entertainment.

A "small" reception would be anything up to forty guests; a "big" one might be anything from one to five hundred. In practice, most people find that once they let their guest list run to more than thirty or forty close friends, it rapidly snowballs up to at least a hundred or more, and this is a situation that may need considerable tact to handle.

A reception in a private house, either the bride's family home or a house lent for the occasion, always has a delightful atmosphere, particularly if, in summer, the garden can be used. But unless a really convenient house is available, it is better to rely upon a hotel or restaurant reception. Third choice, from the point of view of charm and convenience, would be a hired hall with the catering undertaken by an outside firm.

Once the general size and scope of the reception has been decided, and the date booked with the hotel or caterers, the next detail demanding attention is:

PLANNING THE GUEST LIST. Although the bride's mother is the hostess, she will of course include among her guests a number of friends of the bridegroom and his family. The usual procedure is for her to let the groom's mother know approximately how many guests from "his side" can be invited, and whether the list is being limited to close friends only or whether more distant acquaintances can be included; the groom's mother then supplies in writing a list of names and addresses of those she would like invited.

In the normal way, about half the guests are friends of the bride and her family, the other half of the groom's people. Obviously, this can be varied to suit circumstances, if they have a lot of friends in common or if, on the contrary, one of them comes from abroad and can invite only a few people.

The guest list should include both older people, friends of the parents on both sides, and also some younger personal friends of the happy couple. It is not necessary to include children of friends in the invitation, unless one really likes them and wants them to be present; but children of relations ought to be invited along with their parents unless they are very small. Older relatives who live some distance away or are thought to be unlikely to accept, should nevertheless be accorded the courtesy of an invitation. Other people who should not be overlooked are servants of the two families, or former servants with whom they have kept in touch.

Once the guest list is decided and the time and place of ceremony and reception confirmed, the bride's mother can order the engraved or printed invitations (see page 57 for wording and style.) They will need to be sent out at least a month before the wedding date, and six weeks before if possible. It is wise to order just a few more than one expects to need, to be covered against last minute recollections of someone who ought to be asked.

FLORAL DECORATIONS, ETC. Other questions the bride's mother will have to decide a little later, are floral decorations for the reception and music, if any, for the reception, but these need not be settled at the initial conference. If printed Order of Service sheets are to be used, these will need ordering in good time, though not quite so early as the invitations. The bride's mother will also have to decide at an early stage in the proceedings, whether she will invite any relations to stay overnight at her home for the wedding; if so, letters of invitation to them should be sent with the formal invitations to the wedding.

BRIDESMAIDS AND USHERS. The question of bridesmaids and ushers is one to be settled quite early when the general style of the wedding is being decided upon. If there are more than about fifty guests it will almost certainly be necessary to have one or two ushers who can show people to their seats in church and make themselves generally useful at the reception. They should be friends of the groom, or relations of himself or his bride. He must also choose his best man, but this is a matter for himself to settle and not within the scope of the family conference. He would be wise to choose someone of organising ability and character; whether the best man is a bachelor or not is irrelevant.

The choice of bridesmaids is to some extent linked with the size of the wedding as a whole. A girl can have a large and elaborate wedding and only one bridesmaid; but if she has three or more bridesmaids it certainly implies a big and elaborate function.

Traditionally, the bride must invite as bridesmaids, first her own sisters, secondly those of her bridegroom; only after these should she choose friends or more distant relations. This rule of etiquette can cause some heart-searching where a girl has, say, very close friends whom she would like to ask, but is not on very intimate terms with the bridegroom's sister. Nevertheless it is a sound rule to prevent invidious distinctions, and ought to be obeyed.

Only unmarried girls can be bridesmaids; if a sister or close friend is already married, she can be invited to attend as "matron of honour" in which case she usually acts in the capacity of chief bridesmaid, and is dressed slightly differently from any other attendants.

A question sometimes arises as to whether it is possible to have as a bridesmaid a girl of another faith, i.e. whether a Gentile girl friend may be a bridesmaid at a Jewish wedding or a Protestant act as attendant upon a Catholic bride. Often, there is no objection to this arrangement, but if in doubt, the officiating priest should be consulted.

Child attendants can be attractive, but they are also a big responsibility at a wedding. If they are very small, i.e. under seven or so, they usually take part in the processions only, and for the remainder of the ceremony sit in a nearby pew with their mother or nanny, rather than stand throughout the entire service. If there are to be child attendants, the same rules of etiquette apply, i.e. relations have a stronger claim to the honour than friends.

A Guard of Honour lends a pleasing extra touch

of picturesque ceremonial to a wedding, besides being an agreeable way of giving a formal role to friends who might otherwise have no special place in the ceremony. The traditional Guard of Honour is composed of servicemen; but it can be formed by any group of people connected with either the bride or the groom. A party of schoolchildren or Brownies is sometimes seen and looks attractive, but nurses, policemen or women, riders on horseback, or any similar associated group could equally well form the Guard of Honour. The main points are that the members should be uniformly dressed and as smart as possible; they form a double line outside the church door to make an avenue (sometimes with an arch, as of swords or staves) through which the bride and her husband walk when they leave the church; and they can escort her carriage to the reception. During the ceremony at the church, members of the Guard of Honour usually sit together near the back, ready to slip out and take up their places while the register is being signed. They are, of course, invited as guests to the reception.

A WEDDING IN TIME OF MOURNING. Whether the mourning is a family affair or occasioned by some national disaster, important problems of etiquette inevitably arise.

Where the sadness can be foreseen and the wedding planned with that in mind—as in time of war or national dissension—there is no great difficulty. At such times simplicity becomes the fashion and exaggerated formality seems out of place, and the whole function is planned accordingly. In this case all that is said throughout this book about the simple or informal type of wedding, with a small reception only, would be relevant.

When, however, a death or disaster intervenes between the planning of the wedding and the actual day, it is sometimes difficult to know how to proceed. One has the choice of either carrying on with the original plans in full, modifying them as far as possible, or alternatively postponing the whole wedding until such a time as it can be carried out as planned.

To some extent the choice will be settled by circumstance. For instance, if it should unhappily be the parent of the bride or groom, or a brother or sister who dies, then the only real possibilities would be to postpone the wedding for at least three months, or, if that is out of the question, to withdraw the invitations except those to very close friends and relations, to cancel plans for a large reception and have instead a very small informal gathering at home. The latter is the better course—postponing the wedding rather looks as if the bride is determined to have a showy wedding even if she has to wait for it.

Mourning, even the deepest, does not preclude a church marriage, but it should, of course, be a quiet and simple ceremony.

The death of an elderly and distant relation, on the other hand, even if it happened very soon before the wedding, would not nowadays be thought to call for a drastic revision of plans; such a death is today taken to be in the natural order of things and however much one may grieve privately, a public display of grief is not inevitably called for. The situation would normally be met by a few modifications—cancelling the music for the church wedding and ordering entirely white flowers as decorations rather than coloured ones; curtailing the reception in time rather than cutting down on the number of guests, and ordering quieter music for it rather than a series of gay "pop" numbers; and briefing those who will be making speeches, so that they can avoid anything too unsuitably jolly and perhaps make a reference to "how sad we all feel that Great Aunt Emma cannot be here to share this great occasion."

Similarly with national mourning. Anyone who has known the feeling that follows the death of a well-loved monarch or the horror that follows upon, say a local disaster, will realise that it would be impossible to carry on with plans for a big and elaborate wedding within a few days, exactly as if these sad occurrences did not exist. Here again, the situation will usually be met by modifying the arrangements along the lines in the preceding paragraph, and allowing a feeling of simple sincerity to predominate throughout the proceedings, rather than indulging in unsuitable gaiety.

Should one accept an invitation to a wedding if one is oneself in mourning? Here again the answer must depend upon circumstances. The presence of someone known to be in full mourning for a beloved relation or friend is apt to cast a shadow over any social gathering, so if one's personal feelings are not shared by others present, it is perhaps more considerate to withdraw from the occasion. On the other hand if one feels able to go, there is no real reason to refuse. Where one's feelings are really divided, as might happen if, say, one were recently bereaved just at the time of a beloved god-daughter's wedding, one might say or write something as follows: "I feel I must be there when dear Lucy is married to share your rejoicings in her happiness; but I know you will excuse me if I come only to the church" (or, "If I do not stay very long at the reception") "as just now I feel quite unable to be among other people for very long". One would then slip unobtrusively away as soon as one had offered loving congratulations to the bride and bridegroom.

Guests at a wedding in time of mourning should wear dark but elegant clothes. It is quite permissible to wear black at a wedding, but it should not be the total black of deep mourning as this is obviously out of place on such an occasion.

3

Costs of the Wedding

A wedding is usually, though not necessarily, a fairly expensive time, and the main burden of cost falls upon the bride's family and needs to be considered when the initial plans are being made. There are, however, very strong and definite rules which dictate "who pays for what" and in fact these rules are probably the most important in the whole of the wedding etiquette.

They are the most easily grasped if it is understood that they rest upon one assumption: that the girl is the responsibility of her family, and especially of her father, until the moment when she marries and becomes the responsibility of her husband. The mere fact that in these days a great many girls leave the family home long before they marry, and expect to take responsibility (financial and otherwise) for themselves both before and after marriage, does not affect the case!

THE BRIDE'S FAMILY. According to these rules of etiquette, then, the bride's family is responsible for her trousseau and the clothes she wears on the wedding day. (Most probably she will pay for these herself in modern times, of course). They pay for the party or reception following the wedding, and for all the flowers used to decorate the church and reception rooms. They pay for the car which takes the bride to the church for the ceremony, and for any cars hired for guests' use in going from the church to the reception.

The bride's family also pay for the printing of the invitations and if printed orders of service are used they pay for these also. They pay for any flowers in the church, see also page 101. They pay for all newspaper announcements and insertions, and for sending off pieces of wedding cake to friends afterwards. Needless to say, they pay for the cake itself.

THE BRIDEGROOM. The groom is responsible for paying the fees for the actual wedding ceremony, i.e. the clergyman's fee, fee if any for the use of the church, cost of organ, choir and bell-ringers, cost of the marriage licence if used, and fee for the copy of the marriage certificate (often known as "marriage lines"). He pays for the wedding ring, unless of course, a family heirloom one is being used, when it may be provided either by his side of the family or the girl's. He pays for the car which takes himself and his best man to the church, and which takes the bride and groom to the reception. He also pays all expenses of the wedding journey.

The groom pays for the flowers carried by his bride and her attendants at the wedding, and although not obligatory it is "correct" for him to provide floral sprays for his own mother and his mother-in-law to wear. All these flowers will, of course, be ordered in consultation with his bride, to ensure that they are in keeping with the dresses.

He also provides buttonholes for himself, his best man and any ushers. Other menfolk who wish to wear buttonholes (e.g. the bride's or groom's father) usually pay for their own.

BRIDESMAIDS AND USHERS. Expenses of the attendants sometimes provide a problem. The usual arrangement is that each bridesmaid pays for her own dress, but to avoid unnecessary expense this lays upon the bride the obligation of choosing a style for them that will be useful afterwards; if she wants something to fit in with a special scheme, that is unlikely to be of practical use later, then it is more or less incumbent upon her to pay the cost.

Similarly with overnight expenses if bridesmaids have to come from a distance; if they cannot be accommodated in the bride's home, then it may be tactful for the bride's family to pay hotel expenses for them, though this is not obligatory.

Ushers usually pay their own expenses for morning dress if this is worn; also their own travelling and other expenses.

The groom usually gives a present to each bridesmaid, as a memento of the occasion; in choosing these he will have the help of his fiancée. A small piece of jewellery is often given, or a silver ornament, evening bag, or something of that kind. To the best man and ushers he sometimes gives mementoes in the form of cuff-links, cigarette cases, etc.

The groom pays for the traditional "bachelor party" on the eve of the wedding, though this is quite often dispensed with nowadays.

The best man does quite a lot of the actual paying out, at the church for instance, with money given to him for the purpose by the groom.

4

Clothes for the Wedding

Most girls have dreams from early childhood, of how they will appear on their wedding day. And almost every woman, be she bride, mother of the bride, or just a guest, looks upon a wedding as an excuse for appearing at her very best. If everything is to be "just right" on the great day, the clothes of the bridal party will need careful planning and just after the date is fixed, is not too soon to begin.

The costume decided upon by the bride fixes the standard for the rest of the party. Usually morning weddings tend to be simpler, afternoon ones more elaborate. This is not invariable, though, and there are Royal precedents for morning weddings of great ceremony.

Whatever the time of day, if the bride opts for a big and elaborate wedding with three or more attendants and wears white herself, then her bridegroom ought to wear uniform or formal morning dress, and the men of the immediate wedding party (her father and brothers, the men of the groom's family, ushers and best man) should be similarly attired.

If the wedding is a small and not very formal affair, not at a fashionable church, and with a fairly simple reception, then it is in order for the men of the wedding party to wear dark lounge suits even if the bride is in traditional white. But morning dress is becoming more popular even for smaller white weddings.

If the bride is not in the traditional wedding gown and veil, then the men wear either uniform or lounge suits. If however, she is a young widow having a rather formal wedding and wearing a really elaborate dress and hat, then it would be in order for the men to wear morning dress rather than lounge suits.

THE TRADITIONAL WEDDING GOWN. A dress of white or off-white worn with a veil, is the wedding gown tradition. Fashion enters in the matter of style, and even length. The length for a wedding gown is usually the same as for the most formal evening dresses.

The material chosen is often an elaborate and beautiful one—heavy satin, brocade, lace or velvet are all very suitable, depending upon the time of year. At the other end of the scale, bridal dresses of finely-worked organdie and lawn, dotted muslin, or embroidered cotton or fine linen, can look wonderfully attractive. It is really a matter for the individual choice of the bride. One point to bear in mind is the question of whether she wants a dress that is convertible for ordinary use afterwards, or whether it is to be put away in lavender and tissue paper.

In a season when trains are fashionable, the length of train is in direct proportion to the formality of the wedding. Anything over three feet long would only be appropriate for a cathedral ceremony.

Clothes for the bride

The bridal veil may be long or short, and of tulle or lace or both, as the bride prefers. It can be worn with a wreath of orange blossom, a Juliet cap, or a tiara (imitation or real). The tradition of wearing an old family lace veil is a charming one. As old lace is usually quite heavy, the veil will need to be well secured for it to stay in place with modern hair styles. In considering hair style and headdress, bear in mind that it is often possible to arrange for a hairdresser to come to the house to arrange the bride's hair after she is dressed.

Traditionally the bride enters the church with her face covered by her veil, which is thrown back after the ceremony.

A wedding gown should have sleeves and a fairly high neck: ultra-revealing styles are not in good taste. Accessories should match the gown and be as simple as possible; if gloves are worn (they are not obligatory now) a simple, non-transparent style is best. Long gloves should be worn if the sleeves of the dress are short.

Brides who want a white wedding but are not sentimental about keeping their wedding dress, sometimes hire an outfit. This can be a very successful arrangement, and is certainly an economical one. The well-known firms specialising in dress hire are helpful over finding a suitable style and seeing that it fits; if at all possible it is best to pay a personal visit and "book" the outfit in plenty of time, but if a personal call is out of the question, ordering can be done by post or through one of the agents or branches of the firm; in this case one can see sketches of the different dresses available.

Clothes are cleaned in between each hiring and

alterations to make a better fit can usually be done if necessary by arrangement. The hire charge is graded according to the number of times the dress has been used previously. Besides hiring a dress one can buy veil, gloves, jewellery and headdress to complete the outfit. The cost of hiring may be anything between £15.00 and £100.00 according to the outfit chosen, and one is asked to leave a deposit (which may be by cheque) equal to the value of the outfit, returnable when the clothes are taken back.

BRIDESMAIDS' CLOTHES. The bride usually chooses the style for these and plans outfits for her attendants that will harmonise with and set off her own bridal outfit. Since however, the bridesmaids customarily pay for their own outfits, she should be careful not to saddle them with styles or colours which will be unattractive, impractical, or impossibly expensive.

Dresses for adult bridesmaids are normally of the same length as the bride's but less elaborate in style and material. They can be any colour that looks attractive and need not be all the same colour. Shoes are usually plain court shoes dyed to match the dresses, and gloves, if worn, should also match.

Because of the difficulty of finding hat styles to suit a number of girls, flower or feather headdresses are nowadays most popular for bridesmaids, but small feather or ribbon caps can be very pretty and picture hats are such a becoming style that they are never out of fashion for long.

If desired, bridesmaids' dresses can also be hired

and the charges are on approximately the same scale as bridal outfits.

CHILD ATTENDANTS. Little girls can be dressed in similar style to the adults, and can wear either long or short dresses. Pastel colours are usually chosen; if a deeper note of colour is wanted, it is better to introduce it in sashes and trimmings rather than have the whole outfit in it. Sometimes little girls are dressed in period styles such as Kate Greenaway or Victorian costume.

If small boys are included in the bridal cortege, they will have to be young enough not to object to "dressing up." Kate Greenaway styles or replicas of historical uniform are popular for little boys, or a "party style" outfit of trousers and frilly shirt in pastel shades. If a boy is entitled to wear the kilt, ceremonial Highland dress is one of the nicest of all styles, and in this case, of course, the boy can be older than nursery age.

THE MATRON OF HONOUR is usually present only if the bride has a married sister or friend whom she particularly wants to include among her attendants. She usually dresses similarly to the bridesmaids but with a slight difference. She may wear the same colour but made up differently, or the same cut of dress but made in a different colour; or a similar dress but a different headdress.

The matron of honour usually acts as chief bridesmaid.

THE BRIDEGROOM. Unless he is to wear uniform, he will need to consult with his bride about what he should wear. The formality of morning dress, or just a dark lounge suit? For men there is no convenient "half way house" between formality and informality as there is for women, and a definite decision must be taken.

At an elaborate formal wedding, especially if it takes place in the afternoon, morning dress is de rigueur. This means morning coat and light trousers (striped or sponge bag check), grey or black waistcoat, turned-down collar, grey suede gloves, grey topper. If an overcoat is necessary it should be black or dark grey.

The "correct" flower for a buttonhole is a simple carnation, without any greenery, and preferably white; though there are distinguished precedents for breaking this rule and other flowers can be worn if preferred.

BEST MAN AND USHERS. The best man and ushers wear the same as the groom, as do the men of the bride's and groom's families.

In these days few men have much use for formal morning dress except for the occasional wedding in the family, so the hiring of morning dress has become an accepted thing. One can either hire the whole outfit, including shirt, shoes and a tie, or use one's own accessories. If possible it is best to go in person to try on the clothes to be hired, a few weeks in advance of the date when it is needed; the best known of the firms specialising in dress hire have a very wide range of sizes and can give every help and take a lot of trouble in fitting, but it is up to the customer to be fussy; the fit around the collar is one of the most important points to watch. Cost of hiring an outfit of suit, shirt, tie, gloves, is £35.00 or more, and a returnable deposit equal to the value of the outfit will be required.

As hired clothes must be returned promptly if further costs are not to be incurred, it is wise to ask the best man to undertake this job after the wedding on behalf of the groom.

LESS FORMAL WEDDINGS. If the bride decides against the traditional white wedding gown, she still has a wide choice of attractive street-length dresses, with or without a coat according to the weather; or a suit, hat and gloves. It is not an absolute rule to wear a hat or head-covering for a register-office wedding, but it is customary.

For a church wedding, she can wear either a street-length dress or a long dress, which can be quite simple or fairly elaborate; a hat and gloves. The degree of formality will depend upon circumstances; a girl being married for the first time, but having a quiet wedding because, say, of family mourning, might well choose a very simple outfit, whereas a young widow remarrying in church could well wear a really elaborate long dress if she wishes, especially if she is having a big reception afterwards.

In this latter case, the bridesmaids will dress with equal formality to the bride, and the men of the wedding party would also wear formal dress. If the bride, however, is wearing something very simple, the chances are that she will have only one bridesmaid, or at the very most two, and they should wear styles of equal simplicity; the men would then wear informal dress.

If she is not being married in white, a bride can wear more or less any colour she chooses. Black and bright red are usually considered unsuitable for church weddings, and green is often held to be unlucky, but apart from these considerations there are no real rules.

For an informal wedding, the groom wears an ordinary dark lounge suit, or black jacket and striped trousers, with either a bow tie or ordinary tie, black socks and shoes. Nowadays gloves and hats are rarely worn except on a formal occasion. If he wishes to wear a buttonhole, it should, as with formal clothes, be a simple white carnation.

OTHER MEN AT THE WEDDING. The best man, the bride's father and the groom's father, and other men of the immediate wedding party, dress in similar style to the groom. It would be a real breach of convention for any of them to dress with greater or less formality than does the groom. The only exception to these rules is that if any man at a wedding is entitled to wear uniform, he may do so, regardless of how the rest of the group is dressing.

GUESTS AT THE WEDDING. The mother of the bride is, next to her daughter, the most important woman at the wedding and is expected to show this by her choice of dress. The colour is entirely a matter of personal taste and the style chosen will depend upon the size and formality of the wedding, but tradition decrees that she must be beautifully dressed. A street-length outfit is the most usual, but for a very formal wedding a floor length gown can be worn. It should have sleeves and a fairly high neck. The most elegant hat, shoes and gloves she can find, with perhaps a fur, complete the outfit. The gloves should be kept on when receiving guests.

The mother of the bridegroom usually also dresses with a good deal of formality and elegance, along the lines laid down for the mother of the bride.

For guests invited to a wedding, it is sometimes a problem to know how to dress; especially for men, who *must* make a definite decision between formal morning dress and lounge suit.

The time and place of the wedding are a good guide; and so is the size of the reception if one can get any advance information on this. For a wedding at a fashionable church with a reception at a big London hotel after, morning dress would be usual for the men and the women would dress with the utmost possible elegance. For a wedding at a suburban church, even if it is in the afternoon, men not of the immediate wedding party usually need not wear morning dress unless the reception is to be a large and grand one; but the women guests would still wear their prettiest outfits. At a large wedding in the country (the type where friends, and not merely relations, are invited to travel down) morning dress would usually be worn by the men, and correspondingly smart outfits by the women—on the assumption that if the affair is worth going all that way for, it is worth dressing up for it. For smaller country weddings, of course, dress can be quite informal, even a tweed suit not being out of place.

It is quite in order for friends invited to a wedding

to ask "Is it formal dress?" but a tactful and polite reply should convey the necessary information while still making it plain that it is the guest's presence that is wanted and that clothes are a secondary consideration.

THE WEDDING RING. The groom buys this, either in consultation with his fiancée or by himself. If the latter, it is a good plan to ascertain her finger size (it can be done when the engagement ring is being bought) so that later alterations are unnecessary. If an heirloom ring is being used, have it altered to her finger size in good time.

Fashion even enters into the design of wedding rings. In choosing, bear in mind that what looks the height of fashion this year may well look incredibly old-fashioned in ten or twenty years' time. Perhaps the bride will not mind this, but if she does, it is best to choose a simple, timeless style of ring that never looks highly fashionable but never highly unfashionable either.

FLOWERS FOR THE WEDDING. The bridegroom orders and pays for the bouquets carried by his bride and her attendants, and sprays or tiny bouquets for his mother and mother-in-law. They should be ordered in good time and in consultation with the bride, to make sure that they set off and complement the outfits being worn by the various ladies.

"GOING AWAY" CLOTHES. These follow the usual rule of dress, that travel clothes are geared to one's destination rather than one's place of departure. Thus if the bridal couple were flying to the South of France, light, informal cotton or cheesecloth would be appropriate; if travelling to Scotland, tweed might well be chosen and so on. The thing to avoid, at least if one hopes to avoid identification as an obviously honeymoon couple, is the typical "going away outfit" chosen by so many British brides, irrespective of their destination, and consisting of a rather dressy suit and blouse, or pastel dress and coat, and flowery hat; or a new and "citified" suit for the husband.

CLOTHES FOR THE TROUSSEAU. The days have presumably gone for ever when a bride embarked upon her new life with "a dozen of everything." Nowadays, because of rapid changes of fashion and the fact that so many girls go on earning after marriage, she feels well set-up if she has three or four sets of underwear, a dozen pairs of tights, four or five pairs of shoes, a jacket, a coat, a few daytime and one or two evening outfits, the selection depending upon the life she expects to lead, and few girls expect a wardrobe of entirely new clothes. If earning she usually pays for any new clothes herself; otherwise her father does.

5

Invitations

Invitations should be sent out at least four weeks, and preferably six weeks, before the ceremony (giving the hostess time to rectify any "oversights"). They should be sent to all those relations and friends it has been decided to invite, whether or not they are likely to accept.

Invitations are not sent to the parents of the bridegroom nor to his unmarried brothers or sisters living at home—they are supposed to have heard of it by less formal means. A friendly informal letter can be sent as written confirmation of the date and time if this seems necessary.

It is courtesy to invite the clergyman, with his wife, to the reception, although he will probably refuse, except in the case of parishioners whom he knows well. Employees of either family such as farm workers or domestic help are usually invited, and any former employees if the family is still in touch. Business employees need not be invited unless one wishes. To invite business associates is regarded as paying them a special compliment, in allowing them to enter the domain of one's private life.

A list of those to whom invitations are sent should be kept, with space to tick off the acceptances as received. It can usefully be combined with further columns showing wedding presents received and yet another column for ticking these off as they are acknowledged.

Wedding invitations are usually printed or, better still but more expensive, engraved. In the case of a very small wedding with only twenty or thirty guests and a very quiet reception, they could be written by hand, but this is unusual. In such cases a simple, first-person letter of invitation would probably be best.

Engraved invitations are usually done in black script upon a double sheet of good quality white or cream paper; but silver script, or a single card, may be used. The best plan is to consult a good stationer who can show samples of the usual thing. When ordering invitations, remember that fewer will be needed than the actual number of guests, since married couples will be included on one invitation. But order a few above the estimated requirement, to allow for people who may have been overlooked.

Wedding invitations are always drafted in the third person. (See page 57 for styles of wording). If they are to relatives or close friends, they may be accompanied by a short personal letter.

Normally, invitations go out in the name of the bride's parents, who are hosts at her wedding; but if they are not, (if, for instance, they are abroad or are dead) then the invitations should be sent in the name of whoever is acting as host and hostess —perhaps a brother-in-law and sister of the bride, an aunt or even a friend.

Once the invitations have gone out, it often happens that a letter of good wishes, or some small gift, arrives from a not-very-close friend who has not been invited. The question arises: ought so-and-so to have been asked?

If it has been a genuine oversight, by all means send an invitation, however belated. But there is no rule that all well-wishers must be asked to the wedding. One can simply say, or write: "Thank you so much for your good wishes" or "for your present", adding if one wishes, "we do hope you will come and see us in our new home."

WORDING FOR WEDDING INVITATION. The most usual thing is for guests to be invited to both the church ceremony and the reception after. A combined invitation is sent, as follows:

Mr. and Mrs. Reginald Jones
request the pleasure of
the company of
(name or names written in by hand)
at the marriage of their daughter
Kathleen
with
Mr. George Smith
at
St. John's Church, Leyden Bush
on Tuesday, 20th February at 2.30 p.m.
and afterwards at the Manor House Hotel, Leyden.

18 Poll Hill
Leyden Bush — R.S.V.P.

Where the bridegroom is titled, or is a doctor, clergyman, or an officer in the Services, his title is given on the wedding invitation. Any decorations he has won would be used, but not letters signifying degrees or diplomas.

Where several members of the same family are invited to a wedding, unmarried daughters are usually included in the invitation sent to the parents. The names are filled in by hand in the invitation in the following style:

Mr. and Mrs. Reginald Jones
request the pleasure of
the company of
Mr. and Mrs. Laurence Thompson, Miss Thompson and Miss Lesley Thompson.

Unmarried sons, even if living at home, are sent a separate invitation; they should be included on the parents' invitation only if they are young enough to be still at school.

The expression "and Family" should not be used in formal invitations.

INVITATION TO RECEPTION ONLY. If the guests are not invited to the ceremony, either because it is in a register office or in a very small church, the invitations would be worded as follows:

Mr. and Mrs. Reginald Jones
request the pleasure of
the company of
(names)
at the reception to follow the marriage of their daughter
Kathleen
with
Mr. George Smith

At the Manor House Hotel, Leyden
on Tuesday, 20th February at 3 o'clock.
18 Poll Hill
Leyden Bush R.S.V.P.

INVITATION TO THE CEREMONY ONLY. Less often, it happens that friends are invited to the church, but that for some reason, perhaps because of family mourning, there is to be no reception. Then the invitations would read:

Mr. and Mrs. Reginald Jones
request the honour of your presence
at the marriage of their daughter
Kathleen
with
Mr. George Smith
at
St. John's Church, Leyden Bush.
on Tuesday 20th February at 2.30 p.m.
18 Poll Hill,
Leyden Bush R.S.V.P.

The main point to notice about this is that in inviting to a religious ceremony only, one asks for the "honour" of a guest's "presence"—besides being words more in keeping with a religious ceremony, they are slightly more complimentary to the guest who is being asked to turn up without being offered the fun of a party afterwards!

INVITATION TO A DOUBLE WEDDING. This follows the lines of an ordinary invitation, except that the name of the bride who is taking precedence (see page 29) comes first, with her bridegroom, and is followed by that of the other girl and her groom. If two girls who are not sisters have a double wedding, the invitation usually goes out in the name of both sets of parents, and the girl's surnames are given along with their Christian names (in case some guests, who do not know all the families concerned, might assume the parents were divorced.)

If one bride's mother were giving the wedding for both girls, the invitation would read:

Mr. and Mrs. Reginald Jones
request the pleasure of
the company of
(name)
at the marriage of their daughter
Kathleen
with
Mr. George Smith
and of
Mrs. Jones's niece
Norma Wood
with
Mr. Stephen McLean
at
St. John's Church, Leyden Bush
on Tuesday, 20th February at 2.30 p.m.
and afterwards at the Manor House Hotel, Leyden.

18 Poll Hill
Leyden Bush R.S.V.P.

WHEN THE BRIDE'S PARENTS ARE NOT THE HOSTS the wedding invitation should make clear the relationship, e.g.

Mr. and Mrs. Reginald Jones
request the pleasure of
the company of
(name)
at the marriage of Mrs. Jones's god-daughter
Elinor Brown
to
Mr. William Moore
(etc. with details of time and place)

STEP PARENTS. The usual form of a wedding invitation can be used in the case of a step-mother, and the names will be exactly the same. Alternatively, it can be worded.

Mr. and Mrs. Reginald Jones
request the pleasure of
the company of
(name)
at the marriage of
Mr. Jones's daughter
Kathleen etc., etc.

Again, in the case of a step-father, the usual invitation can be used, or an alternative form making the relationship clear, can be used instead.

Mr. and Mrs. Reginald Jones
request the pleasure of
the company of
(name)
at the marriage of
Mrs. Jones's daughter
Kathleen Hutchinson etc., etc.

WHERE PARENTS ARE DIVORCED. If the bride lives with her mother, the mother issues the invitations. If she lives with her father, and her mother is quite out of the picture, her father and step-mother issue the invitations. But generally, the bride's mother should send the invitations—firstly, because the father takes the same role, whoever gives the wedding, and also because it is better for a man to appear as a guest at his ex-wife's reception, than for her to appear at his.

If the mother has married again, her daughter's surname should be given in the invitations as it will be different from the mother's.

If the daughter is living with the father, and he has married again, the invitation will usually be issued by himself and his new wife. If the wedding is given by the father in this way, the bride's own mother (if present at all) should be given the first pew. If the mother is giving the wedding, the bride's father should give the bride away.

THE INFORMAL INVITATION. If engraved invitations are decided against for any reason, the invitations would be in the form of a letter from the mother of the bride:

Dear Mrs. Martin,

My daughter Kathleen is to be married on Tuesday, February 20th to Mr. George Smith. Because of the recent death of George's brother, only a few intimate friends will be present. May we ask you and Mr. Martin to give us the pleasure of your company? The ceremony is at 2.30 p.m. at St. John's Church.

We hope you will be able to come back with us to tea afterwards.

Yours sincerely,
Bertha Jones

THE SECOND MARRIAGE. If a widow is young, invitations are sent out in the name of her parents, just as if this were her first marriage; the only difference is that her married name is added:

Mr. and Mrs. Reginald Jones
request the pleasure of
the company of
(name)
at the marriage of their daughter
Kathleen Montgomery
with
etc., etc.

If the widow is not so young and the invitations are sent out by a friend, they could read as follows:

Mr. and Mrs. Norman Robinson
request the pleasure of
the company of
(name)
at the marriage of
Mrs. John Golding
and
Mr. Frederick Warburton
at
etc., etc.

A widow may send invitations to her wedding in her own name:

Newspaper announcements

Mrs. John Golding
requests the pleasure of
the company of
(name)
at
St. Paul's Church, Hartfield
at
12 noon
on
Friday, 9th August
on the occasion of her marriage
with
Mr. Frederick Warburton

The Old Vicarage
Hartfield R.S.V.P.

NEWSPAPER ANNOUNCEMENTS. Sometimes a small and quiet wedding is announced to friends through the press. The insertion is put in the Forthcoming Marriages column and is worded on these lines:

Mr. G. Smith and Miss K. Jones

The marriage arranged between Mr. George Smith and Miss Kathleen Jones will take place at St. John's Church, Leyden Bush, on Tuesday, February 20th at 2.30 p.m. No reception, owing to family mourning, but friends will be welcome at the church.

RECALLING WEDDING INVITATIONS. An engagement may be broken after invitations have gone out, or illness or death in the family may make it necessary to postpone or recall invitations. Guests should be notified immediately. The notice sent to them should give some indication of the reason for the change. If time allows, notice recalling an invitation should be printed or engraved in the same style as the original invitation.

Examples:

Mr. and Mrs. Reginald Jones
announce that the marriage of their daughter
Kathleen
to
Mr. George Smith
will not now take place.

or, for a postponement:

Mr. and Mrs. Reginald Jones
announce that owing to the illness of Mr. Smith
the marriage of their daughter
Kathleen
with
Mr. George Smith
has been postponed indefinitely.

Or, if the invitations are cancelled because of family mourning:

Mr. and Mrs. Reginald Jones
regret exceedingly
that owing to the recent death of
the mother of Mrs. Jones
the invitations to the marriage of their
daughter
Kathleen
with
Mr. George Smith
must be cancelled.

18 Poll Hill
Leyden Bush

Replying to invitations

REPLYING TO WEDDING INVITATIONS. Recipients of wedding invitations should reply within two or three days. For a formal invitation the reply should be in the same third person style, as follows:

Mr. and Mrs. Laurence Thompson have much pleasure in accepting the kind invitation of Mr. and Mrs. Jones to the marriage of their daughter on Tuesday, 20th February at St. John's Church and afterwards at the Manor House Hotel.

If only one of the recipients can accept, it should read:

Mrs. Laurence Thompson has much pleasure in accepting the kind invitation of Mr. and Mrs. Jones to the marriage of their daughter on Tuesday, 20th February at St. John's Church and afterwards at the Manor House Hotel. Mr. Thompson much regrets that as he will be out of town on business, he will be unable to be present.

Where an invitation is declined, there is no need to recapitulate details of time and place. For example:

Mr. and Mrs. Laurence Thompson thank Mr. and Mrs. Reginald Jones for their kind invitation to the marriage of their daughter Kathleen, but much regret that they are unable to accept, owing to a previous engagement.

6

Wedding Presents

Once the invitations to the wedding have been sent, presents will begin to arrive, and one of the most important rules of wedding etiquette must be observed: that each present must be acknowledged, promptly, by letter and in her own hand, by the bride. Another rule of etiquette is that everyone who accepts an invitation to the reception should send a present of some kind, not necessarily expensive.

If the bride is wise, she will keep a careful list of presents as they arrive, ticking them off as acknowledged. It is a sound rule to write the "thank-you" letters on the day each gift arrives; even if this entails writing a dozen or more letters on some days, it is still easier than letting them accumulate. If there is to be a very large number of wedding guests, it may be impossible for the bride to acknowledge each present as received; in this case it is best to enlist the help of her chief bridesmaid in sending off formal acknowledgements that presents have arrived safely, but proper letters of thanks must all be sent off by three weeks after the wedding.

Are the presents to be exhibited at the reception? If so, the cards should be carefully attached to each gift as it is unwrapped, because they must be displayed together. Otherwise it is often easier to send the wedding presents straight on to the new home before unwrapping, and unpack them there, minimising risk of loss or breakage.

Exhibiting the wedding presents, whether at the reception or informally at the home of the bride for any friends who care to "drop in", is much less obligatory than it once was, probably because presents now run to all kinds of items such as a living-room carpet, a refrigerator, or a set of garden tools or washing-up equipment, which hardly lend themselves to elegant display!

If presents are to be on show, it is usually on long trestle tables (at a reception, placed down one side of the room, or grouped at the end, or in a separate small room) covered with white cloths. (Good quality sheets can be used for this). Large items like a vacuum cleaner or long mirror can be grouped on the floor at the end of the table. The card of the donor should be placed with each gift, and care should be taken to display everything to advantage; if several table lamps are received, for instance, they should be spread among the other things, not all grouped together. Cheques are not displayed, but a typed list of people who have sent cheques or money (*not* mentioning the amounts) together with any gifts which cannot be displayed (e.g. "From the Bride's Parents—a House") can be placed on the table with the other presents.

WHAT PRESENT TO GIVE. The old joke about the bride receiving a dozen salt cellars and no pepper pot has largely lost its sting in these practical days. The modern way is for the bride and groom to compile a list of things they would like to be given and for anyone in doubt to ask to see the list. This is not mercenary, but merely the modern angle on courtesy —it is a politeness to donors not to allow them to waste their money on something useless and to ensure that they really do give as much happiness as they intend.

The list can be as detailed as one wishes (for instance, if tableware is being asked for, details of pattern and style should be given), but it should include a number of modestly priced items dotted about among the more expensive things. Household linen is often included on the list nowadays—this is no longer necessarily the traditional gift from the bride's mother, as it once was.

If the bride is herself shy of seeming to "ask" for special presents, her mother can take charge of the whole business of circulating the list to enquirers. It is advisable to have two or three copies of it to show people, but if more copies are in circulation, the whole object is defeated.

There is, however, no rule that a present-giver must be guided by the list or must even buy something new; often a gift of a piece of silver or nice old china from one's own collection forms a very acceptable present.

Some brides prefer to hand over the whole business of the wedding-present list to one or other of the big stores which runs this kind of wedding-consultant service. Inquiries are then told simply "Harridges have the list of what we want". Advantages of this method are that it takes a lot of trouble off the bride and her mother, and that it can be helpful to friends who live far from the big shopping centres, and that things can be sent back later and changed if necessary. But some people find it a rather cold-bloodedly commercial approach to the subject; and some givers may feel that they are being induced to spend more than they had planned, or feel a certain resentment at being directed where to shop.

Wedding presents are usually sent to the bride before the ceremony (people who are friends of the groom, or who know both the man and the girl, can include a card saying "With every good wish to you both", or something of that kind). Any sent after the wedding, are addressed to the couple jointly. Friends of the groom alone can, if they prefer, send a present to him direct; in which case it is his job to acknowledge it. Any such gifts should, of course, be included with the others on show if there is a display of wedding presents. Where transport problems arise (if the couple are going to live some distance away after their wedding) it may be more practical to have presents sent direct to the new home.

SUGGESTED ARTICLES FOR WEDDING PRESENTS. The following list represents the basic equipment needed for a young couple to start a home.

It is not intended to be exhaustive, as individual needs and ideas differ so widely as to what constitutes a well-equipped home. It is simply intended to provide a guide to the sort of things most young married couples will need at the outset of starting a home, and hence a list of items that one could appropriately give, or ask for, as wedding presents.

Linen: 1 best tablecloth
1 kitchen tablecloth

6 table mats
6 table napkins
4 tea towels
4 kitchen towels
4 dusters
1 oven cloth
2 traycloths
4 hand towels
4 guest towels
4 bath towels
4 face cloths
2 bath mats
1 continental quilt for each bed
2 continental quilt covers for each bed
4 blankets
1 bedspread for each bed
2 pillows for each bed
3 pillow cases for each bed
2 fitted bottom sheets for each bed
2 top sheets for each bed

TABLEWARE AND CUTLERY. This can nowadays be bought either in half dozens or in "place settings". The latter is a practical and economical way of building up one's equipment from small beginnings, but if the new household will be having many visitors, then "half-dozens" or even "dozens" of things such as sherry glasses, may well be more use. In any case, the new bride should aim at bringing her equipment up to the following minimum as soon as possible:

China, glass and cutlery

6 dinner plates
6 small forks

Wedding presents

- 6 pudding plates
- 6 side or tea plates
- 1 meat dish
- 2 vegetable dishes
- 6 small bowls for fruit or cereals
- 1 large bowl, china or glass
- Coffee pot
- 6 coffee cups and saucers
- Carving set
- 6 large knives
- 6 small knives
- 6 large forks
- 6 tablespoons
- 6 pudding spoons
- 6 soup spoons
- 6 tea spoons
- Butter dish and knife
- 6 cups
- 6 saucers
- 1 teapot, milk jug & sugar basin
- 1 sauce boat
- 1 cruet
- 6 tumblers and jug
- 6 all-purpose wine glasses
- 6 sherry glasses

Kitchen equipment

- Set of 3 saucepans
- Frying pan
- Kettle
- Measuring jug
- Scales
- Cake tins
- Set of fireproof dishes
- Meat tins
- Colander
- Strainer
- Pastryboard and rolling pin
- Bread board and knife
- Egg whisk
- Cook's knives
- Corkscrew
- Lemon squeezer
- Bread, cake and flour tins
- Washing-up equipment

Electrical equipment

- Iron
- Radio
- Clock
- Vacuum cleaner
- Refrigerator
- Electric fire
- Table or standard lamps
- Record player
- Television set

Washing machine
Coffee percolator
Electric mixer, grinder and blender
Kettle and/or teamaker

Miscellaneous

Ironing board
Carpet sweeper
Garden tools
Lawn mower
Plate rack
Trays
Cigarette box
Rugs
Mrs. Beeton's Cookery and Household Management
Items of furniture
Soda siphon
Garden chairs
Picnic set
Pictures
Ashtrays
Bookcase

EXCHANGING WEDDING PRESENTS. If the business of the wedding present list has been carefully managed, it should not be necessary to consider exchanging many gifts, but it can occasionally happen that one is given, say, a pink table-lamp for a room that one had planned to be entirely blue. Can one ask for it to be exchanged? There is no conclusive answer and each case must be judged on its merits. With old friends, or kindly souls who are unlikely to take offence, one can of course be quite frank and say "Would you mind very much if we asked the shop to change it?" People who are old-fashioned, or sticklers for convention, or very proud of their personal taste, might be offended at being asked this, and it might be better to forget the whole thing.

7

The Legal Aspect

When the bride has decided what kind of a wedding she hopes for, arrangements will have to be made with whoever is to officiate at the ceremony, and this should be done well in advance.

TIME AND PLACE FOR THE WEDDING. According to English law a marriage may take place upon any day of the year, but some religious groups have certain restrictions (see page 26).

Marriages in a church, chapel or before a registrar, may take place at any time between 8 a.m. and 6 p.m. Two exceptions to this are marriages by Special Licence, which may take place at any hour, and Jewish marriages, which may take place at any time of day and in any building approved by the Jewish authorities; even, at times, in a private house. Quaker marriages are also allowed to take place at any hour and in any building, including a private house, that has been regularly used as a place for Quaker worship for at least a year.

MARRIAGE ACCORDING TO THE RITES OF THE CHURCH OF ENGLAND. To be legal, a marriage in church must be either by Banns, by Licence, or by Superintendent Registrar's Certificate. It is not limited to parishioners or practising church members. The parish church of the district is the usual one for the marriage of people who are not regular church-goers; those who are, are usually married at whichever church they attend, provided they have their names entered on the electoral roll of that church (if it is not their own parish church). When non-church people apply to be married, the clergyman would wish to make sure that they do at least understand the teaching of the Church on the question of marriage, and exactly what it is they will be promising when they marry.

MARRIAGE BY BANNS. This is the cheapest and most popular, and has the most ancient tradition. Banns are the public announcement that two people wish to marry and an invitation to anyone knowing just cause or impediment to the union to declare it. It means that the names of the couple are read aloud, during the morning or evening service, on three Sundays prior to the marriage (usually consecutive though not necessarily so) in the parish where they live and are to be married. If they live in different parishes, the banns must be read in both places, and the clergyman whose church is not being used for the marriage must send a certificate (cost £2.50) that the banns have been duly read, to the clergyman whose church is to be used for the marriage. The actual cost of the banns themselves is £4.50 in each church where they are called.

Before reading out the banns, the clergyman will ascertain that the couple are aged 18 or over or, if under 18, that they have the consent of their parents to the marriage.

When the banns have been read three times, the couple are at liberty to marry any time within the next three months; if longer elapses, the banns will have to be read again.

The fees for a marriage after banns are £37.00 if the couple live in the same parish and £43.00 if they live in different parishes. Should the couple wish to marry at a church other than their local parish church, they may do so if it is the usual place of worship of one or both of them and their names are entered on the electoral roll, but in this case they will need to get certificates from their parish church or churches saying that the banns have been duly called (such certificates cost £2.50 each).

Where one party lives in Scotland or Ireland, the banns are published in the place of residence according to local usage and in the usual way in England in the place where the other party lives. If one party lives in Wales the procedure is the same as if they lived in England.

MARRIAGE BY LICENCE. This is of two kinds, by Common Licence or by Special Licence. Couples are usually married by Common Licence and a Special Licence (costing £40.00 if applied for in person and £46.00 if applied for by post) is granted only in exceptional circumstances.

A Common Licence, granted by the Bishop or Archbishop through their Surrogates, means that the marriage can take place, without banns, in the parish of one of the parties, or in the church regularly attended by one of them provided they are on the electoral roll.

One of the parties must apply in person for the licence, and he or she will have to sign a declaration on oath, stating that there is no legal reason why the marriage cannot take place (a wilful false statement is a criminal offence and could result in a prosecution) and also that one of the parties to the marriage has lived for the fifteen days immediately preceding application for a licence, within the parish in which the place chosen for the ceremony is situated (or, alternatively, that one of them is on the Electoral Roll of the church chosen and is a regular worshipper there). In the case of people under 18, the necessary permission to marry, signed by both parents or legal guardians, must be produced in writing.

With a Common Licence, the marriage may take place as soon as it is issued, without further notice, and at any time within the next three months. After that a fresh licence would be required.

The cost of a licence is usually £26.00, and the fees for a marriage by licence are £36.00.

A Common Licence may be obtained from a Surrogate and is issued on the authority of the Diocesan Bishop. Often he is the local clergyman; or if not, any clergyman can supply the names of surrogates. He can take the oath and transact the business with the Registrar of the diocese in which the church is situated. In many cases he will issue the licence at once.

The charge for the copy of the "marriage lines" is £2.50—whether one has been married by banns or by licence.

SPECIAL LICENCES. In special circumstances where the ordinary methods of solemnisation of matrimony cannot be used, (e.g. where one of the parties is too ill to attend in church, or has been unexpectedly ordered abroad at very short notice) a Special Licence can be issued from the Registrar of the Court of Faculties, 1 The Sanctuary, London SW1P 3JT, by the Archbishop of Canterbury.

Where such a licence is granted, the marriage may take place in an unlicensed building—a hospital, private house, or a cathedral, church or chapel which has no licence for marriages in the ordinary way; and it can take place at any time of day. It must still be performed before witnesses by an ordained priest and be according to the rites of the Church of England.

The third and least well-known way of getting married in church is by:

SUPERINTENDENT REGISTRAR'S CERTIFICATE. This is more often used for non-conformist marriages than for Church of England ceremonies. It takes the place of having the banns called, for one of the parties must make a declaration before the registrar of the district where they live, that there is no legal objection to the marriage and that the consent of parents (in the case of minors) has been obtained. If they live in different districts, each must make the declaration in his or her own district. A false declaration can lead to a prosecution for perjury. The person must have lived in the district for seven days prior to making this declaration. If only one party has fulfilled the residential qualification, he or she must give the notice, and the other party must be living in England or Wales when the notice is given.

Providing that the Superintendent Registrar is satisfied with the information given, he will make an entry in his notice book, (for which a fee of £8.00 is charged) which is then on public display for twenty-one days, at the end of which he will issue a certificate for the marriage to take place at any time within the next three calendar months from the date of giving the notice.

MARRIAGE AT A REGISTER OFFICE. If the bride does not wish to marry in a church, the ceremony may take place at a Register Office. In this case it is usual for it to be attended by only a very few close friends or near relations, two of whom will act as witnesses; or there may just be the two witnesses, who need not be known to the couple or to one another.

Marriage at a Register Office can be either by licence or by certificate, and will take place in the presence of the Registrar or his deputy.

If the marriage is to be by certificate, the procedure for obtaining this is just as described opposite, for getting married in church by Superintendent Registrar's Certificate.

If the marriage is to be by licence, the residential qualifications for obtaining this are the same as for a licence to marry in church, but instead of applying to the Bishop or his Surrogate. one makes application to the Superintendent Registrar. One party must apply in person and make a similar declaration to that outlined above under the heading of marriages in church by Common Licence. The Registrar will issue the licence after one clear day has elapsed and the marriage may then take place at any time within the next three months Sundays, Christmas Day and Good Friday excepted. For a list of the various fees for marriage at a Register Office by certificate or licence contact the General Register Office, St Catherines House, 10 Kingsway, London WC2B 6JP, or your local Register Office.

MARRIAGE WITH RELIGIOUS RITES NOT THOSE OF THE CHURCH OF ENGLAND. Marriage according to the rites of all other religious sects in England, other than the established Church, is usually by Superintendent Registrar's Certificate, either with or without a Superintendent Registrar's licence in addition. In a few cases it may be necessary for the Registrar of Marriages to be present, if the minister himself is not authorised by law to perform the duties of the registrar.

The marriage must generally take place at a place of worship within the district where one or other of the couple lives, or else at their usual place of worship. It must be solemnised between 8 a.m. and 6 p.m. with open doors and in the presence of at least two witnesses. It can be according to the rites and usages customary for the particular religious sect of which the couple are members, but to comply with the law the couple must at some point in the service each make a declaration that he or she takes the other to be his lawful wedded wife or husband. Jewish weddings can be celebrated according to Jewish rites in a synagogue or private house, and it need not be within the district where the parties live.

MARRIAGE UNDER THE REGISTRAR GENERAL'S LICENCE. Where the parties do not wish to be married according to the rites of the Church of England and one of them is so seriously ill that the ordinary methods of solemnisation cannot be used, they may be able to obtain a Registrar General's licence. This allows the marriage to take place at any time and in any convenient place.

MARRIAGE OF DIVORCED PERSON. A divorced person must produce the decree of divorce when he or she wishes to remarry.

English law allows such remarriage, but the Anglican church forbids it, so no clergyman of the Church of England or of the Church in Wales can be compelled to solemnise the marriage or permit it to be solemnised in the church of which he is a minister. Very occasionally a clergyman is willing to do so in special circumstances.

A person who has been through a form of marriage and subsequently been granted a decree of *nullity* in respect of it is regarded as unmarried and free to marry in church. The decree of nullity should be produced to the clergyman.

No divorced person may remarry, even in a register office, until the "decree absolute" has been granted. It must be applied for by the successful petitioner six weeks after the issue of the "decree nisi".

Apart from these provisions, marriage for divorced persons follows the legal requirements set out previously, i.e. a licence or certificate will be needed, the residential qualifications must be fulfilled, and so on.

A divorced person or a widow or widower who is under the age of 18 may remarry without parental consent.

Marriages in Scotland

MARRIAGES IN SCOTLAND. Scottish law provides that young people over 16 may marry without parental consent. Marriages may be solemnised by a Minister of Religion, or an authorised registrar. No prior residence is required for a marriage in Scotland. All marriages must be preceded by notice of marriage being given by both parties to the registrar of the district in which the marriage is to take place. After the expiry of 15 days from the giving of the notice the registrar will complete and issue a marriage schedule which in the case of a religious marriage must be given to the minister at the ceremony. The cost for the marriage notice is £4.00 per person.

The civil marriage ceremony requires two witnesses to be present and costs £12.00 plus £2.00 for a copy of the entry in the marriage register—the "marriage lines". After one month has elapsed the marriage lines cost £5.00.

All persons giving notice of marriage must produce to the registrar their birth certificate, and if they have been married previously, documentary proof of the termination of that marriage, i.e. divorce or death certificate.

A person domiciled outside Britain must produce a certificate of no impediment to marriage issued by a competent authority in his or her own country. This requirement does not apply if the person has resided in Britain for two years or more at the time of giving notice.

MARRIAGES OF BRITISH SUBJECTS ABROAD. The Foreign Marriages Acts 1892 and 1947 make special provision for marriages abroad of British subjects or parties one of whom is a British subject. Such marriages, sometimes called "Consular marriages", are solemnised by a British consul or other "marriage officer" authorised under the Acts and have the same legal effects as if duly solemnised in Britain.

It is always advisable for parties proposing to marry abroad to consult the nearest British Embassy, Legation or Consulate.

MARRIAGES OF MEMBERS OF BRITISH FORCES SERVING ABROAD. The Foreign Marriages Acts also provide for marriages abroad, where at least one of the parties is a member of the Forces serving abroad, to be solemnised by a chaplain to the Forces or by a person authorised by the appropriate Commanding Officer. The Commanding Officer must give a certificate that he has no objections to the marriage and it must be solemnised before two witnesses. Such marriages have the same effects as if duly solemnised in Britain.

FOREIGN MARRIAGES. Under the British Nationality Act of 1948, a British woman does not now lose her British nationality by reason of her marriage to a foreign national. Conversely, an alien woman who marries a British subject does not automatically acquire British nationality; she has to go through the process of naturalisation and registration.

A British marriage ceremony is not necessarily valid in every foreign country, and anyone intending to marry a national of another country is most strongly advised to consult the Consul or other representative here of that country, to make sure the legal requirements of that country are complied with.

MARRIAGE BY PROXY. This is not permissible under English law. It is, however, recognised by certain other countries, so that it is possible for someone resident in England to be married by proxy, in a perfectly legal manner, in one of those countries, and such a marriage will, in general, be recognised by English law. Here again, the Consul or representative of the country concerned, should be consulted to make sure that all the proper formalities are complied with and to safeguard one's legal position.

NAVAL MARRIAGES. Difficulties over publication of banns, which might arise in the case of serving members of the Royal Navy, were dealt with by Parliament in 1908. The commanding officer or chaplain can either publish the banns (in the case of a Church of England wedding) or issue a certificate of registration after the lapse of 21 clear days after the giving of notice (in the case of a wedding to take place in a nonconformist chapel or register office). Notice must be given in the usual way to a registrar in the district where the other party lives, or else the banns must be called in church in the usual way.

OTHER LEGAL PROBLEMS.

Passports. A bride can have an existing passport amended to her married name by completing Forms G and PD3 and by the minister or registrar to perform the ceremony completing PD2. Leaflet

PD1 gives full information. If she has no passport the bride may obtain one in her married name by completing Form A, sending it with the necessary enclosures and Forms PD2 and 3 as above, to the appropriate passport office.

Alternatively, either partner may apply for a family passport. Any application should be made at least six weeks ahead. The passport is sent to the applicant post-dated to the date of the marriage.

Wills. Marriage automatically cancels existing wills made by either of the couple, unless the will was expressly made in contemplation of this particular marriage. Therefore, if there is enough property involved to make it seem immediately urgent, a fresh will should be made either before the wedding (and it should be stated therein that the marriage is contemplated) or as soon afterwards as practicable.

Marriage Settlements. A marriage settlement is a contract legally entered into by the parties before marriage, containing detailed stipulations in regard to the ownership, division and control of their respective fortunes and property, real and personal, after marriage. They are usually only entered into in cases in which considerable property is involved, where the normal provisions of common law regarding the property of husbands and wives would be inadequate to secure the desired safeguards.

The bride's father, if wealthy, often makes a marriage settlement, to provide for his daughter should the husband land in financial difficulties. Usually the bride may not touch the capital.

Other legal problems

Legal Obligations of a Married Couple. Once married, a husband and wife acquire legal obligations to one another. The husband is legally obliged to maintain his wife and any children they may have, in a state commensurate with his own means. The wife, however, even if a woman of means, or like so many modern brides, earning an income of her own, is not actually obliged to maintain her husband—unless he should become destitute and a charge upon the State, in which case she would be obliged to contribute to his maintenance.

A wife is usually legally regarded as her husband's "agent" for purposes of housekeeping and running the home, so that any reasonable expenses she incurs, such as bills for food, are his legal responsibility, and any savings she is able to make from her housekeeping money belong to him also. But he is not liable for extravagant luxuries such as clothes or jewellery over and above what is reasonable and necessary for her in her position as his wife.

There is no legal ruling as to how much a husband should allow his wife for housekeeping and other expenses, or whether she should receive any personal allowance. She is not legally entitled to know his income, though he will usually know hers as he has to state his wife's income as well as his own in making his tax return. He is liable to pay the tax on her income as well as his own, but the wise modern couple will, of course, allow for this in planning their joint expenditure.

The law also has something to say on the subject of the choice of a home. At one time the husband had the absolute right to choose where the couple should live, but this is so no longer, and nowadays, from the legal point of view, each partner is entitled to an equal voice in the matter. But from the human point of view, the wise wife will still recognise that a man's home is often determined by his need to be near his work, and will agree to this, even if it means she has to go to a district she would not have chosen otherwise.

It is quite usual for a house to be bought either in the name of the wife, or of the couple jointly, even when the husband provides the actual purchase money. The house that is in the name of the wife does actually belong to her, even if the husband has paid for it; the same applies to any securities or savings certificates bought by the husband in his wife's name, or to money he may pay into her separate banking account. In these days it is most usual for a young couple to buy their first house by means of a mortgage, and this can often best be done by combining the mortgage arrangement with life insurance cover, which ensures that should the husband die before the payments are completed, the wife is not saddled with the burden of completing the payments in addition to all her other worries.

After marriage a woman continues to be personally liable for any debts and obligations she may have contracted before marriage. And if she trades by herself in business, she is subject to the bankruptcy laws in respect of her separate property, just as if she were unmarried.

Hire Purchase. The Hire Purchase Act 1965 rules that before agreements are entered into over articles whose cost does not exceed certain stated sums the seller must state in writing to the hire-purchaser, a price at which the goods may be bought for cash. The Act also provides that any agreement for hire-purchase implies that the goods are fit for their required purpose. Furthermore, the seller cannot retake possession of the goods, except by action in the Courts, when over a third of the hire purchase price has been paid.

Because of the complications of the Act, however, it is really advisable to seek professional legal advice if the hirer is threatened with seizure of goods or is involved in any dispute concerning his agreement.

Those who enter into hire purchase agreements are most strongly advised to read any documents relating to the transaction with the utmost care.

It is generally known, but perhaps worth re-stating here, that goods bought on hire purchase may not be re-sold until the first hire purchase transaction is completed.

PROHIBITED MARRIAGES. Marriage is not allowed between certain people who are more or less distantly related already. These are the rules:

A man may not marry his

Mother
Adoptive mother
Former adoptive mother
Daughter
Adoptive daughter
Former adoptive daughter
Father's mother
Mother's mother
Son's daughter
Daughter's daughter

Sister
Wife's mother
Wife's daughter
Father's wife
Son's wife
Father's father's wife
Mother's father's wife
Wife's father's mother
Wife's mother's mother
Wife's son's daughter
Wife's daughter's daughter
Son's son's wife
Daughter's son's wife
Father's sister
Mother's sister
Brother's daughter
Sister's daughter

A woman may not marry her

Father
Adoptive father
Former adoptive father
Son
Adoptive son
Former adoptive son
Father's father
Mother's father
Son's son
Daughter's son
Brother
Husband's father
Husband's son
Mother's husband
Daughter's husband

Prohibited marriages

Father's mother's husband
Mother's mother's husband
Husband's father's father
Husband's mother's father
Husband's son's son
Husband's daughter's son
Son's daughter's husband
Daughter's daughter's husband
Father's brother
Mother's brother
Brother's son
Sister's son

Statutory Exceptions from Prohibited Degrees of Relationship

A man may marry his

Former wife's sister
Brother's former wife
Former wife's brother's daughter
Former wife's sister's daughter
Former father's brother's wife
Former mother's brother's wife
Former wife's father's sister
Former wife's mother's sister
Former brother's son's wife
Former sister's son's wife

A woman may marry her

Former sister's husband
Former husband's brother
Former father's sister's husband
Former mother's sister's husband
Former husband's brother's son
Former husband's sister's son
Former brother's daughter's husband

Former sister's daughter's husband
Former husband's father's brother
Former husband's mother's brother

Note: In these lists the terms "brother" and "sister" include a brother or sister of the half-blood.

There is no law prohibiting the marriage of first cousins, but it is sensible to consult your doctor in case of any inherited disease or disability.

WHEN A MARRIAGE IS NOT VALID. A marriage can actually take place and still be legally held not valid, i.e. not to exist at all, in certain conditions. These are:

Where either party is a minor under 16 years.
Persons within the prohibited degrees of relationship as given above.
Persons married to a living partner and whose marriage has not been ended by divorce.
Where a party lacks capacity to give valid consent.

A marriage where one or both parties, being of an age where parental consent is needed, have made a false statement about his or her age and married without parental consent, is still legally valid. The person who makes such a false statement is, however, committing a criminal offence for which he or she can be punished.

8

A Church of England Wedding

The traditional Church of England wedding, as conducted for centuries past in this country, is a singularly beautiful ceremony and as has been said earlier, it is the right of any couple who wish for it—excepting, of course, for divorced people. Even if the wedding is to be a simple and quiet affair, with only a few close friends present and no special clothes or other efforts at "show", the church ceremony, with its exchange of solemn vows and its appeal to God to bless the couple, is still far more meaningful and impressive than any civil ceremony can possibly be.

If a church wedding is chosen, the bride and groom usually go together to see the vicar or rector by appointment. The points they will need to discuss with him at this first interview are outlined on pages 27–29.

If the ceremony is to be a big and elaborate one, a rehearsal is sometimes held on the preceding day, so that everyone may feel confident and happy in their roles. But for the ordinary wedding this is unnecessary. *It is, however, recommended that those in the immediate wedding party should read through the service as set out in the Prayer Book, beforehand,* so as to be well prepared and understand what they are called upon to do. This may sound obvious, but it is surprising how often this simple preparation is neglected.

On the day of the wedding, the ushers will arrive first of all, to be ready to show people to their places. The guests should aim to arrive at the church about fifteen to twenty minutes before the time given on their invitations (which is, of course, the time of the bride's arrival). On arrival they will usually be greeted by one of the ushers. The usual formula for placing people in church is "friends of the bride on the left of the aisle, of the bridegroom on the right", but this can be varied if necessary.

The bride's mother should provide the ushers with a list of the most important guests, who will be accommodated in the pews nearest the front, and she should arrange that a sufficient number of seats is left for them; otherwise earlier comers may get the better seats. The front pews of all are left for the immediate families of the bride and bridegroom, and pews immediately behind, for their other relations.

The bridegroom arrives with the best man twenty minutes to half an hour before the bride is due to arrive. They usually deposit their hats in the vestry, and this is the time for the best man to attend to payments to organist and choir, bell-ringers and any others who have fees due. A good tip to the verger is never amiss; he can unobtrusively do a good deal to make things go smoothly and if confetti is thrown, it is he who will have to tackle the sweeping up.

They then return to the church and take up their positions at the top of the aisle, just level with the front pew, and slightly to the right of the aisle centre.

A Church of England Wedding

Bridesmaids arrive about a quarter of an hour before the bride, and wait at the church entrance (or just inside the porch if the weather is cold or wet); while waiting they can make any last-minute adjustments to their flowers or hair, and arrange themselves in the order in which they will follow the bride when she arrives. If there are child attendants, mothers or elder sisters usually wait with them during this period, and slip into church themselves only when the procession is just ready to start.

If there is a choir, they usually walk in procession to the church porch to meet the bride there at the moment of her arrival and walk ahead of her up the aisle.

The organist will be playing soft "opening voluntaries" until the bride arrives, when at a pre-arranged signal from the porch, he switches to a wedding march and the procession starts up the aisle; the clergyman and choir leading, followed by the bride on the right arm of her father or whoever is giving her away, then her train-bearer or child attendants if any, and finally the adult bridesmaids, with the chief bridesmaid on the left of the first pair.

The bride's father, if he is leading the procession, will need to walk with a certain measured tread, neither too fast nor too slow. (It is worth practising.) As he reaches the chancel steps where the clergyman will be waiting, he moves slightly to the left, to bring his daughter opposite the priest's right hand; the bridegroom, who has turned to watch his bride as she comes up the aisle, now taking up his position opposite the left hand of the priest, with his best man to the right of him.

This is the moment for the bride to hand her

bouquet to the chief bridesmaid and also to take off gloves if she is wearing them.

Throughout the ceremony, the bridesmaids remain standing in the positions in which they are now. Any child attendants under the age of seven or so can be taken into the pews alongside their parents or sisters, if the strain of standing still so long might be too much for them. They are returned into the procession later, at the moment when all the bridesmaids move off to accompany the bride to the vestry for the signing of the register.

The clergyman now begins to read the prayer-book ceremony beginning with a passage setting forth the importance and purpose of marriage from the Christian point of view, and goes on to ask, for the final time, that if anyone should know of any impediment to the marriage, they must now declare it. Then he asks first the man and then the woman if they freely consent to the marriage and intend to fulfil the obligations of a husband and wife; to which they each reply "I will".

At this point the actual ceremony of joining them in matrimony begins, with the clergyman asking the question "Who giveth this woman to be married to this man?" or the modern equivalent.

There is widespread misunderstanding about the response to this question. The bride's father does *not* reply "I do". He makes no spoken reply, but simply takes the right hand of his daughter and gives it to the priest (not to the groom, as many people seem to believe; the old idea was that the parents gave the girl to the Church and the Church gave her to her bridegroom).

The clergyman then joins the couple's right hands

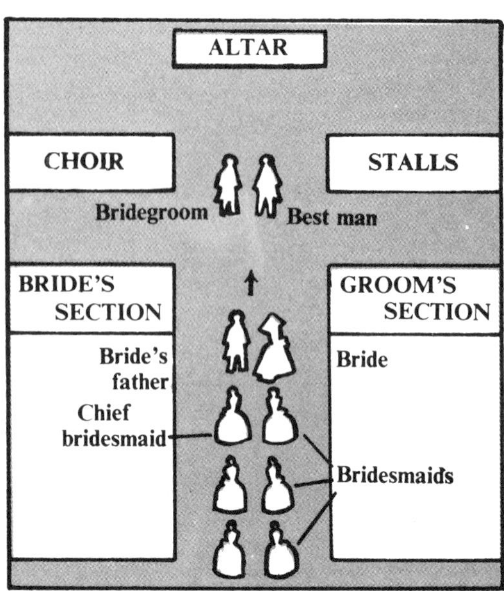

Forming the bridal procession

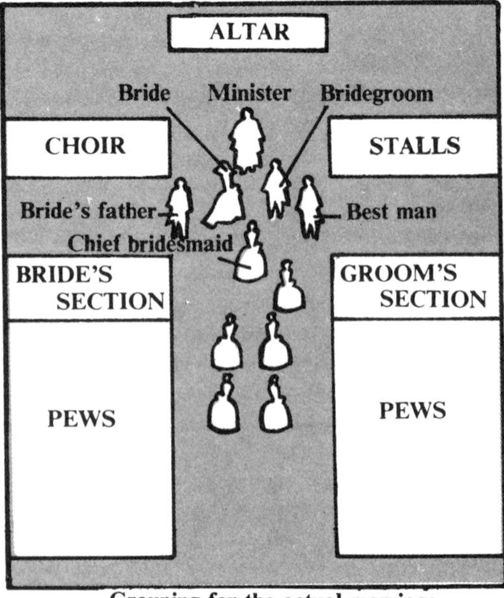

Grouping for the actual marriage

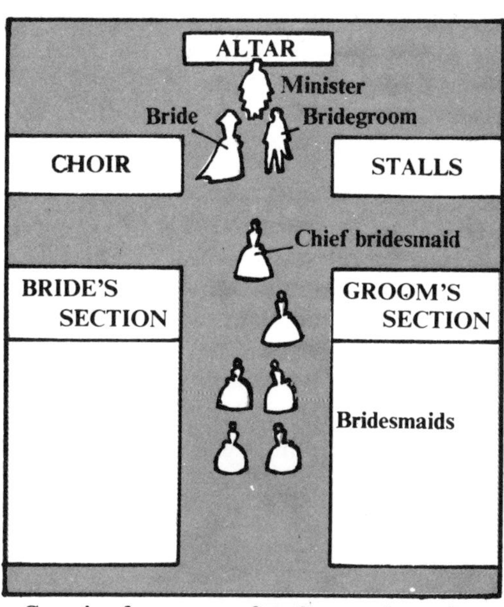

Grouping for prayers after the actual marriage

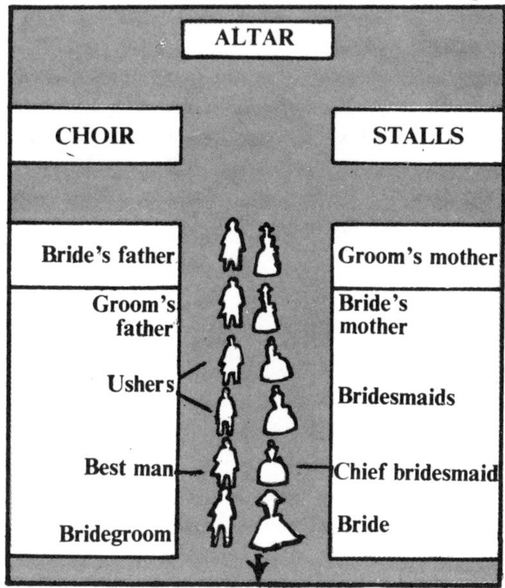

Grouping for the recessional

and they make their vows to one another, prompted by the clergyman.

After the bride's father has given her away, he usually steps back a pace or two and then moves unobtrusively into the front pew alongside his wife.

Now comes the moment when the ring is produced. The bridegroom may keep it himself in a pocket beforehand, or he may give it to the best man to look after for him; there is no special rule to be observed. It is a sound idea, however, for the best man to have a second, very cheap, ring in reserve, just in case the real ring cannot be found at the right moment.

The ring is placed upon the bible held by the clergyman and he blesses it. Then the groom again takes the ring, places it upon the third finger of his bride's left hand and makes his final vow to her, again prompted by the priest. Then after a prayer that the couple may have divine assistance in keeping these solemn vows, the priest again joins their hands and pronounces them man and wife. In a church wedding, this is the actual moment of marriage, although in a register office wedding they are husband and wife from the moment the vows are exchanged.

More husbands wear wedding rings nowadays than formerly, and the Series 3 ceremony makes provision for the bride to give the groom a a ring. The Series 1 marriage service does not, so in this ceremony the ring may be given privately in the vestry afterwards, or the wife can slip it on her husband's finger, without words, immediately after her own ring has been put on.

If this latter course is chosen, the matter should be mentioned to the clergyman before the ceremony, so that he can allow a brief pause for this before going on with the service. In this case the chief bridesmaid can look after the ring for the bride during the earliest part of the service, and produce it at the moment the groom is producing the other ring.

After the ceremony with the ring, the bride and groom are asked to kneel, the best man moves back to a pew, and the rest of those present remain standing. Kneeling is something the bride and groom should rehearse beforehand, for it is not easy to kneel gracefully in a long dress, and the bridegroom should assist the bride both on kneeling down and on rising, by placing his hand under her elbow. The kneeling posture should be an upright one, with just the head bent.

Next comes a psalm, usually sung as an anthem by the choir if there is one, final prayers, a hymn if the wedding is choral, and sometimes an address.

Immediately the ceremony is over, the newly-married pair, with their bridal retinue and immediate relations, proceed to the vestry to sign the church's marriage register and receive a certified copy of the entry (the "marriage lines"). The clergyman usually signs first, followed by the bride, who signs her maiden name for the last time, the bridegroom, and two witnesses, usually the best man and the chief bridesmaid or alternatively two of the parents. It should be arranged beforehand who are to be the witnesses.

One small problem often throws a very long shadow over what should be a happy time, and that is, where one or other of the couple has some fact about their parentage which they might prefer to keep hidden and which they feel may be openly revealed in this signing of the register. In this case the best course is to confide in the officiating clergyman and he can often arrange for the relevant part of the register to be "accidentally" covered by a blotting paper so that nothing is apparent. (It is, needless to say, unwise to conceal true facts from one's intended marriage partner: this suggested precaution is merely to prevent such facts coming to the notice of outsiders.)

After the signing of the register, there is usually a certain amount of kissing and congratulation all round, and the best man will slip out of the vestry by a side door to summon the bridal car, and the clergyman will be thanked and said goodbye to, if he is not attending the reception. Then the procession re-forms at the entrance of the vestry —bride and groom leading (bride on her groom's left arm), followed by the chief bridesmaid and best man, bridesmaids and ushers, the parents (cross-paired) and other relations who may have gone to the vestry.

During the signing of the register, other guests will have remained in their places, either talking very quietly or listening to the organ music or an anthem from the choir. When the procession is ready to re-enter the church, the organist moves into a bridal march, everyone stands, and the happy pair move down the aisle again, acknowledging their friends with smiles.

If there is not to be a reception, it is often possible for the bride and groom to receive their friends at the back of the church, or in the church garden, but permission of the clergyman must first be obtained. If this is done, the receiving line would be the same as for an ordinary reception (see page 136).

Whether there is a reception or not, there is often a pause outside the church, during which the bride and groom pose for photographs; they should not, however, be greeted formally or engaged in conversation, and should move on to the reception in their car as soon as possible. After them in order go the bride's mother with the groom's father, groom's mother with bride's father, bridal attendants, other guests, and finally, the ushers and best man.

EXTRAS AT A CHURCH WEDDING. If special flowers are wanted, or any awning or carpet at the entrance, the clergyman should be consulted. The church will normally have a hiring fee for awning and carpet, but flowers are the responsibility of the bride's mother, who can either do them herself from home, or arrange with a florist. But the clergyman must be consulted first. Flowers are not usually allowed in churches in Lent.

If there is to be anything unusual about the order of service, or special hymns, service sheets are usually printed (in silver upon white paper) for distribution to the congregation. Any good stationers or printers could advise about the style.

A modern idea is to have the service video-tape recorded, so that the happy couple can view it again and re-live it afterwards. If this is to be done, the clergyman should be consulted first for permission. The same applies to the taking of photographs actually inside the church.

The arrangement of a Guard of Honour is dealt with on page 36.

Confetti cannot now be thrown outside the churchyard premises, as this is a contravention of the Litter Act. Some churches prohibit its use inside the churchyard, others have no objection. It is as well to ascertain this point beforehand.

MUSIC FOR A CHURCH WEDDING. Choice of music for the organ and choir can be either left entirely to the organist (who can usually be relied upon to choose something suitable); or, if the bride wishes, she can specify music of her own choice, provided of course, she does not ask for something completely secular and unsuitable, or something so difficult that it would need special rehearsal and has consulted with the priest.

Hymns specifically suitable for the marriage service include:

"Love, divine, all loves excelling"
"Oh, perfect Love"
"Oh, Father all-creating"
"The voice that breathed o'er Eden"

and others in the "Holy Matrimony" section of the hymnbook. But there is no rule that specifically wedding hymns must be used and if the bride prefers, she can have one of her favourite hymns instead. Among the general hymns very often sung at weddings are:

"Praise my soul the King of Heaven"
"God be in my head"
"The King of Love my Shepherd is".

Music for a church wedding

For the arrival of the bride, the Lohengrin "Bridal Chorus" by Wagner is virtually traditional, and for the final procession, the Mendelssohn "Midsummer Night's Dream" Wedding March. But here again there is nothing against the bride choosing something else if she prefers. Before the service the following would be suitable:

- "Jesu Joy of Man's Desiring" (often also sung as a wedding anthem)
- "In Dir Ist Freude" or any other of Bach's Choral Preludes
- Purcell's Prelude in G
- The Aria from Handel's 10th Organ Concerto
- Couperin's "Soeur Monique".

Possible alternatives for the final procession are:

- Handel's Minuet from "Berenice"
- Purcell's Trumpet Voluntary
- Guilmant's "Spring Song".

9

The Roman Catholic Marriage Ceremony

The couple who go through the Roman Catholic marriage ceremony are linking their lives together in a most solemn and enduring way. For this reason, it is most important to read the marriage service carefully beforehand.

Once a Catholic couple have decided to get married in church it is wise for them to go to see their priest as soon as possible—six or even nine months before the proposed wedding day. This enables the Church to arrange for "Information for Marriage" instruction to be given, during which the meaning of the ceremony and the various options open to the couple will be thoroughly discussed. Now is the time for the couple to ask if any prayers, readings, hymns and blessings that they both particularly like can be included in the marriage service. It also provides an opportunity for the priest to complete the necessary forms showing that the couple are free to marry, and that they go along with the church's understanding of what their marriage means.

If the marriage is to be a "Mixed Marriage", i.e. between a Roman Catholic and a non-Catholic, even longer notice may be needed for two reasons; firstly because a Dispensation is required (to be obtained from the parish priest of the Catholic party) and secondly because in England, the usual rule is that the non-Catholic should have several periods of instruction from the priest, in order to help him or her to understand fully what is involved in marriage with a member of the Catholic faith.

A parish priest (or dean in his absence), can grant the Dispensation in England or Wales. He cannot refuse, but if he has doubts may refer it to the bishop.

For the priest to be able to grant the dispensation, the Catholic partner has to make a twofold "promise", a formal expression of his religious conviction, as follows: "I declare that I am ready, as God's law demands, to preserve my Catholic faith and to avoid all dangers of falling away from it. Moreover, I sincerely undertake that I will, as God's law also requires, do all in my power to have all the children of our marriage baptized and brought up in the Catholic Church." The non-Catholic partner does not make a promise.

A Catholic marriage requires an authorised priest (or deacon) and two witnesses. There are two forms of marriage ceremony: the Rite of Marriage during Mass; and the Rite of Marriage outside of Mass. The first is usual where both partners are Catholic and may be used when one partner is a baptized non-Catholic, but not if one partner is not baptized. However it may be preferred, for a mixed marriage, to have a ceremony of the second form, the Rite of Marriage without a Nuptial Mass, because non-Catholics are in general not admitted by the Catholic church to take Holy Communion in a Catholic ceremony. Thus a mixed marriage with a Nuptial Mass would possibly mean that one partner's family and friends could not take part fully in the service. The choice of ceremony should therefore be discussed with the priest and the two families. If the parish priest agrees, a non-Catholic minister may be invited to take part in a mixed-marriage ceremony, in "choir dress".

The service should be read through beforehand.

The time of the Nuptial Mass should be discussed and agreed with the priest. Whatever time is arranged, it should be borne in mind that for those who are to receive Holy Communion, this will mean fasting for one hour before Communion.

Parishioners can be married at their own parish church without special fee, but for a wedding at one of the fashionable churches, a fee is usually charged to non-parishioners. An offering is usually made to the priest who conducts the marriage, and is given to him in a sealed envelope afterwards.

Whatever ceremonial is decided upon, invitations are sent to chosen guests in the usual way and, of course, these need not be limited to members of the Roman Catholic Faith. Guests assemble at the church in good time and if there are to be many of them, ushers should be appointed to show people to their places. Bride's family and friends to the left, bridegroom's to the right, is the usual custom, but there is no absolute rule; it is, however, wise to arrange that some places at the front are reserved for families and most important guests, and the ushers should be provided with a list of these.

Bridegroom and best man arrive about twenty minutes before the ceremony and this is the best time to go to the Sacristy to attend to payments of fees to the organist, etc. (The parish priest will advise about such fees.) They then return to the church to wait at the sanctuary steps for the arrival of the bride.

The bridesmaids arrive at the church about a quarter of an hour before the bride and wait inside the porch, arranging themselves in the order in which they will follow the bride when she arrives. Any child attendants are usually looked after by their mothers or sisters or by the older girls during this period. If there is a choir, they walk in procession to the church porch in readiness to precede the bride up the aisle on her arrival.

The bride arrives with her father and he escorts her up the aisle to where the groom is waiting, then after the priest has inquired of the man and the woman if they will each take the other in marriage, the bride's father gives her away by putting her hand in the priest's; the couple repeat their marriage vows after the priest. The bride's father meanwhile moves quietly back to take his place beside his wife in the front pew.

In the Catholic ceremony there is no mention of "obedience" on the part of the wife. After the couple have taken their vows, the priest says "You have declared your consent before the Church. May the Lord in his goodness strengthen your consent and fill you both with his blessings. What God has joined together, let no man put asunder".

Then follows the blessing and giving of the ring(s). The bride gives her bouquet to the chief bridesmaid, and gloves if she has worn them. Many couples prefer a double ring ceremony, others have only one. The best man usually looks after the ring(s) and produces them when the priest indicates. The priest then blesses the ring(s).

The Roman Catholic Wedding

The groom takes the ring and says "(name), take this ring as a sign of my love and fidelity". Putting the ring on the bride's left thumb he says "In the name of the Father"; putting it on the index finger, "and of the Son"; on the second finger "and of the Holy Spirit"; and finally on the third finger when he says "Amen".

If the bride is giving a ring to the groom she would repeat this action and words.

Bidding prayers and the Nuptial Blessing follow, possibly Holy Communion and Thanksgiving, then the final blessing and dismissal. The newly married couple, together with the two witnesses, go to sign the civil register, during which the congregation may sing a hymn. (A copy of the register entry costs £2.00.) If the wedding has been a simple one without Mass, the bridal couple go with their attendants and immediate families to the Sacristy for this, but if there is a Mass to follow, the bride and groom go with the two witnesses (usually members of their families) to the Sacristy, and the bridal attendants return in a procession to the pews reserved for them at the front of the church and join with the other members of the congregation in following the procedure of the Mass when it is celebrated.

For the Nuptial Mass, the bride and bridegroom return to kneel within the Sanctuary; if the bride is wearing a veil or train which presents difficulty in managing, one of her attendants remains with her to help during the Mass. The bridegroom also gives her assistance when it comes to kneeling or rising (not easy to manage gracefully in a long gown) and it may be as well for them to practise this beforehand.

If Holy Communion is to be received by the Catholic attendants, or by any members of the bride's or bridegroom's families, they will rise at the proper time and come forward to where Holy Communion is administered by the priest, after which they return to their pews.

At the conclusion of the Mass, the bride and bridegroom leave the sanctuary, with the bride walking on the left of her husband. The attendants leave the pews to walk behind them down the aisle, the chief bridesmaid walking with the best man and after them the bridesmaids in pairs. The guests leave after them, the most important guests such as close relations being allowed by the others to move away first.

If, for a big wedding, special flowers are wanted, or if an awning or carpet is wanted at the entrance, the parish priest should be consulted.

Choice of music can either be left entirely to the organist, or the couple can ask for music of their own choice, provided they decide upon something suitable.

10

The Nonconformist Ceremony

Marriage at most non-conformist churches is by Superintendent Registrar's Certificate (see page 78). Usually the church or chapel has been registered as a place for marriage, and in this case the minister will perform the duties of a registrar in keeping the marriage register as well as performing the ceremony. If the church or chapel is not registered, however, a registrar of marriages will have to be present.

If the normal place of worship of either party is not in the district of his or her residence, the marriage may take place in the normal place of worship, providing it is not more than two miles from the boundary of the district in which the notice is given. If there is no suitable registered building in the districts in which the two parties live, the wedding may take place in a suitable registered building in the nearest district.

If a Registrar's presence is required at a marriage in a building which *is* registered for marriages, this fact must be mentioned to the minister and his consent obtained, when notice of the marriage is given.

The marriage may be solemnised according to such form or ceremony as the parties think fit, providing that in some part of the ceremony they each declare that they take one another for husband and wife.

A significant feature of most Free Church orders of marriage is that anything suggesting the old-fashioned idea of subservience of the wife to the husband is eliminated. The wife is not asked to obey; the service is based upon the idea of an equal partnership and she is not asked to do anything that her husband is not asked to do.

Although each of the separate denominations has its own Order of Marriage, most of them follow to a greater or lesser extent upon the service as used in the Church of England; a reading of Chapter 8 of this book will be helpful, but in planning a marriage according to nonconformist usage it is also strongly advised that the marriage service as used by the denomination in question should be carefully read beforehand.

11

The Quaker Ceremony

Marriages conducted according to the usage of the Society of Friends (Quakers) are not confined to those who are actually in membership. Anyone who is a regular attender at Quaker Meetings for Worship and who is in agreement with the Quaker testimony as to the nature and character of marriage, may apply to the Registering Officer of the Monthly Meeting of the area in which they wish the marriage to take place for permission to be married according to Quaker usage. Such application must be made whether the couple are Friends or merely Attenders, and it should be made at least six weeks before the proposed date of the marriage; in the case of non-Friends it will need to be supported by the written recommendation of two adult members of the Society of Friends.

The certificate of the Superintendent Registrar will be needed; see page 78.

Public notice is then given of the proposed marriage at the appropriate Meeting for Worship; this is the equivalent of calling the Banns in a Church of England ceremony. Providing no objection is raised, the Monthly Meeting will then arrange for a special Meeting for Worship for the solemnisation of marriage, and will arrange that a sufficient number of Friends will attend at such a meeting, in order that it may be rightly held in accordance with Quaker custom, as it is probable that a number of the invited guests will have little notion how such a meeting is conducted.

The meeting will be held in whatever is the usual place for Meeting for Worship in that area —it can be in the traditional Quaker Meeting House, but if none exists, the marriage can equally take place in a schoolroom, private house, or wherever the ordinary Quaker Meeting for Worship has been held for the past twelve months. Public notice of a Meeting appointed for the solemnisation of marriage must be given at the place at which it is to be held at the close of the usual Meeting for Worship last held there before the day of the marriage.

It is usual for a number of non-Quaker friends of the couple to be invited to a Quaker wedding, and for this reason it is advisable to have one or two ushers, as at a church wedding, who arrive first and show people where to sit.

The bride and groom sit together, facing the meeting, with the bridesmaids, if any, and best man on either side of them, their close families usually near at hand.

There is no very strong custom either way about the dress of a Quaker bride. Many women choose to wear the traditional white wedding dress and veil of any English bride, and to have one or more prettily-dressed bridesmaids; others prefer to be married in ordinary day clothes. But whatever the bride wears, morning dress for the men is hardly ever worn among the Society of Friends. Dark or grey suits with carnation buttonholes are the usual thing.

It is customary to decorate the meeting-room with vases of flowers, and this is in the hands of the bride's mother, who can either arrange them herself or call in a florist.

There is no pre-arranged music or singing at a wedding in the Society of Friends.

Because of the presence of a number of non-Friends who are unused to the method of silent worship, a meeting for the solemnisation of a marriage usually lasts only half an hour or perhaps forty-five minutes. It can, however, be longer if the couple wish.

The Society of Friends publishes a small leaflet explaining just how a Quaker marriage is conducted; it is a good idea to include these with the invitations sent to non-Friends, to give them some idea what to expect.

The meeting proceeds along the lines of the normal Quaker Meeting, with those present either remaining in silent worship or speaking, as they feel moved to do so. At some point early on in the meeting, bride and groom stand, take one another by the hand, and declare as follows, the man usually speaking first:

> Friends, I take this my friend (name) to be my wife promising through divine assistance to be unto her a loving and faithful husband, until it shall please the Lord by death to separate us.

The bride then makes a similar declaration, saying "wife" and "husband" where appropriate.

Alternatively, the words of the promise may be slightly varied, as follows:

> Friends, I take this my friend (name) to be my wife, promising through divine assistance and so long as we both on earth shall live, to be unto her a loving and faithful husband.

The words "through divine assistance" may be replaced by "with God's help".

The bride then makes a promise in the same form, changing the words "husband" and "wife".

Either of these two forms of promise may be used, but no other form may be used, and both husband and wife use the same form. Which form it is to be, is agreed beforehand between the couple, and the Elders of the Meeting.

The Quaker ceremony allows no special moment for the putting on of the bride's ring. Usually it is done immediately after the promises have been exchanged; alternatively, and almost as usual, it is put on at the conclusion of the Meeting for Worship and at the time the register is signed.

After the declarations, the meeting continues as it began, with a period of silent communion of spirit, in which help may come from a vocal prayer or from spoken messages appropriate to the occasion; and those present seek the divine blessing upon the newly-wedded pair and their home. At the end of the appointed time, a handshake between two of the Elders gives the signal that the meeting is at an end.

Immediately after (or sometimes during the meeting, though this is less frequent nowadays) a marriage certificate prepared beforehand is signed by the couple and by two witnesses. It is then read aloud; and signed by all those present, to be kept by the couple as a memento of the occasion.

The Quaker ceremony

The marriage is also registered by the Registering Officer in his duplicate-register book; this entry is signed by the bride and groom, two witnesses, and the Registering Officer, and fulfils legal requirements.

If the marriage has taken place at a Friends Meeting House which has adjoining rooms available, as many have, the reception usually takes place there at once, and all who have been present at the meeting are invited to attend it—even if, as may happen (since this has been a public meeting for worship) they may not be personally known to the couple. Catering is in the hands of the bride's family to arrange as they think best. Bearing in mind the Quaker views, alcoholic drinks are not usually served at a wedding reception held in Meeting House premises.

Alternatively, the reception may take place at the home of the bride's parents, or at some room hired for the occasion. In this case, usually only those specially invited to do so, go on to the place of the reception.

12

The Jewish Ceremony

A Jewish marriage is solemnised generally in a synagogue. Civil law, however, permits the solemnisation in any building and at any time of day.

In all cases, before the Jewish religious ceremony of marriage is performed, the parties must obtain and produce the certificate of the Superintendent Registrar for Marriages of the district (or districts) in which they live, permitting the marriage either by certificate or by licence.

Alternatively, in the cases where the parties have already married civilly at a Register Office, they must produce their marriage certificate before the Jewish religious marriage can be solemnised.

In addition to the requirements of Civil law being fulfilled, if the marriage is to be solemnised at or through an orthodox synagogue, the parties must obtain the authorisation of the Chief Rabbi. Application for this should be made through synagogue officials of the district where the couple live. The marriage authorisation costs £15.00.

A Jewish wedding does not need to be lavish or expensive, as is sometimes thought.

Parties to a Jewish marriage must both be Jews. If one of them is not of Jewish birth, evidence of proselytisation will need to be produced when applying for the marriage authorisation. The bridegroom must be a member of the synagogue.

Because of formalities, application for the marriage authorisation should be made at least four weeks before the proposed date of marriage.

As in civil law, so in Jewish religious law, some marriages are prohibited; as for instance, where the parties are within certain degrees of consanguinity or where one or other of the parties is under some other disqualification laid down in religious law. The minister of the synagogue or the office of the Chief Rabbi should be consulted.

There is no objection to the remarriage of divorced persons in Jewish law, provided the divorce has been recognised by Jewish law first.

A Jewish wedding may not take place on the Sabbath (sunset Friday till sunset Saturday) nor on festivals and certain other specified days.

On the Sabbath prior to the wedding-day the bridegroom and his father, and the father of the bride and other close relatives of the couple may attend divine service at the synagogue and the bridegroom and nearest relations will be given the honour of being called up to the reading of the weekly portion or lesson from the Pentateuch. The bride should visit the *mikveh* before the wedding.

An orthodox bride and bridegroom usually fast on their wedding-day in expiation of past sins, and offer special prayers so entering upon their new life encouraged and fortified by the knowledge that they do so with divine grace.

The bride usually wears a white or off-white dress with long sleeves and a veil. She wears no jewellery, not even her engagement ring. The bridegroom and all men attending the orthodox or Reform synagogue must wear hats. In orthodox synagogues women too should have their heads covered. See Chapter 4 for guests' style of dress.

Guests arrive in good time and are shown to their places by ushers. The bridegroom arrives before the bride, and his male escort accompanies him; this includes his father and other male person "giving him away", his bride's father or other male person "giving her away" and his best man. They are given the most prominent pew. The groom may, alternatively, be escorted by the two fathers (and the bride by the two mothers).

An outstanding feature of Jewish weddings is the rectangular canopy of *chuppah* made of silk or velvet and supported upon four poles about five or six feet apart. It symbolises the home which the bridal couple are about to set up and its frailty reminds them of their own weakness and of their dependence upon divine guidance and help and that they must so live as to deserve and enjoy these if their home is to be secure. Alternatively a *tallit* (shawl-like wrap used in prayer) may be used, held aloft by four men, one at each corner.

When the bride arrives, the bridegroom is conducted under the canopy. The male escort then leaves the synagogue to bring in the ladies; the bride coming on the arm of her father or whoever is "giving her away", and following her in procession are the bridesmaids and the two mothers of the bridal couple escorted either by their husbands or other close relatives.

The bride stands on the right of the bridegroom, the bridesmaids behind, and the men in the procession stand beside the groom, the women beside the bride. In the Reform and Liberal synagogues, the women and their escorts are not separated but stand together under the canopy on each side of the bridal couple. The bridal party under the canopy faces the Ark, which is on the east side of the synagogue, with the officiating minister or ministers facing them.

The marriage ceremony should be in the presence of at least a *minyan*, i.e. a quorum of ten adult males.

If the marriage takes place out of the synagogue, the procedure is similar.

The service opens with a blessing of welcome from the Psalms pronounced by the Minister and/or the choir and this is followed by a Psalm of Thanksgiving and an address to the bridal pair. Following this the minister pronounces the betrothal blessing. The bridegroom then places a ring on the first finger of the bride's right hand and declares to the bride:

"Behold, thou art consecrated unto me by this ring according to the law of Moses and of Israel." The bride makes no corresponding verbal promise in Jewish ceremonial—her acceptance of the bridegroom's declaration, and the ring, is held to constitute her side of the promise; and with this the marriage is complete.

In some synagogues, before the bridegroom gives the bride the ring, the minister, addressing both parties, says "You, (name), and you, (name), are about to be wedded according to the law of Moses and of Israel. Will you, (name of bridegroom, take this woman, (name of bride), to be your wife? Will you be a true and faithful husband unto her? Will you protect and support her? Will you love, honour and cherish her?"

The bridegroom replies "I will".

Then the minister turns to the woman and repeats the question in similar terms, and she replies "I will".

In synagogues where these questions do not come as part of the marriage ceremony, they will be put more informally before the actual ceremony.

In orthodox synagogues the *ketubah* or marriage contract is then read in Aramaic and in English.

Next come some words of benediction, and then a glass is placed on the floor before the bridegroom who breaks it under foot. This symbolises the frailty of things in life and reminds the bridal couple in the midst of their joy that sad events also exist in life, and that against such breaches in life, their home, symbolised by the canopy, must be so conducted as to earn divine protection.

Special psalms may be introduced into the service. This should be discussed with synagogue officials, as should the question of floral decorations.

The wedding fees should be discussed with the synagogue secretary. These are between £50.00 and £150 but they can be reduced if they are beyond the means of the couple or whoever is paying for the wedding.

If the bride and groom have not already married at a Register Office, now, in conclusion, they sign the marriage registers of the synagogue and two witnesses and the synagogue's Secretary for Marriages also sign, as does the officiating minister. The procession then leaves the synagogue, and goes on to the reception.

13

Planning the Wedding Reception

The wedding reception is the responsibility of the bride's parents or nearest relations, who act as hosts on this occasion. It can be large or small, formal or informal, lavish or simple, according to taste and circumstances.

The only absolute necessities for a "correct" wedding reception are:

1. The bride's mother and father, or whichever relation or friend is giving the reception for her, should stand just inside the entrance to welcome guests as they arrive and before they move on to greet the bride and groom.
2. There must be something in which to drink a toast to the happy pair, and someone to make a short and if possible witty speech proposing their health, to which the bridegroom will reply. There need not necessarily be any other speeches. Wine is the most usual thing in which to drink healths, but soft drinks are in order if preferred.
3. There should be a wedding cake for the bride to cut. It can be quite small, made and iced at home, but it should be the traditional rich fruit cake with almond paste and hard white icing.

Given these three essentials, a small reception in a suburban drawing room, with only a dozen guests, can be quite as correct and enjoyable as the lavish affair for a thousand people in some gilded London hotel.

In actual fact of course, most brides have a reception somewhere between these two extremes, and it is in knowing "where to draw the line" that problems of etiquette and planning arise.

Practical considerations settle some of the questions. If people will be making a fairly long journey to the wedding, then a time around midday or early afternoon will be best and this in turn will dictate whether they must be provided with a luncheon meal at the reception (if the wedding takes place before 1 o'clock). On the other hand, a midday wedding to which people have not travelled far can perfectly well be followed by a buffet luncheon, and in many ways this is an attractive plan as it allows guests to move around and circulate.

Or, if the wedding is in the afternoon, then a still lighter buffet meal would be provided, with tea and small cakes and biscuits as well as a few sandwiches and savouries. Less usual, but quite as correct, in the case of a late afternoon wedding, would be a reception that approximated to a cocktail party, lasting a comparatively short time, and with the emphasis on drinks accompanied by a few canapés and savouries rather than on buffet or tea-time food. A small sherry party reception is also often arranged to follow a small and quiet morning wedding.

There is no set rule about how long the reception lasts. Its actual formal end comes when the bride and groom leave for their honeymoon journey; often they leave after an hour or so; but sometimes there is music and dancing in which the newly-married pair join, and which may go on for three or four hours or even longer.

To some extent the time occupied by the reception will be dictated by the number of guests. If there are several hundreds, it will take a long time for them all to file past and greet the bride and groom. At the smaller wedding with say a hundred or so guests, it is etiquette for the bride and groom to move around the room, either separately or together, after the formal reception and have a further few words with each of those present, and this again takes a certain amount of time. The speeches and healths will occupy about twenty minutes to half an hour, and this should be allowed for in planning.

The next thing to plan is where the reception shall be held. The nicest kind of reception is that held in a private house, but with most families this will limit the numbers it is possible to invite. If a really big house is available, either the bride's own home or perhaps a house lent by a godmother or aunt, then quite a large reception can be given, but the average small town house would be suitable only for a reception limited to not more than thirty people. Another drawback to the private-house reception is that it entails a lot more work for the bride's mother in her capacity as hostess. She will have to arrange the hiring of glass, china and cutlery, deal with the florist, the caterers, the wine merchants, the agency supplying staff and one supplying a band or hiring a stereo set; see that there are enough chairs and tables, that the cloakroom arrangements are adequate . . . and have the responsibility of the clearing up afterwards.

Probably the most trouble-free plan, for a reception of any size, is to book a large room, or suite of rooms, at a good hotel which can also see to the catering and arrange the whole thing at an inclusive charge of so much per guest. It is usually also arranged for the bride and groom to use rooms in the hotel in which to change their clothes during the reception. If a good hotel, which is accustomed to such things, is chosen, the manager will be able from experience to smooth out many of the details for the bride's mother.

Failing either of these alternatives, it may be necessary to book a local hall, but this combines the drawbacks of the first two: it has not the intimate atmosphere of a private house, and the hostess still has all the organising to do. The main advantage is that it does make it possible to invite a good many guests. If booking a hall, remember to plan where the bride and groom will change their clothes.

If the reception is to be elsewhere than at home, bookings will have to be put in hand early—very early if the wedding is to be in late spring or summer months.

One small point to be settled when deciding the place for the reception is—will there be someone to announce the guests by name on arrival or will this formality be dispensed with? Either is quite usual.

Whatever the locale decided upon, the bride's mother will be well advised to call on firms of caterers, etc., as much as possible rather than attempt to do everything herself. A really good organiser who enjoys planning a party might possibly manage to give a simple wedding reception for up to thirty people in a private house without outside help; but the specialist firms who do this kind of thing as a matter of routine are better able to foresee and forestall snags. Also, she must remember that she will have many other pre-occupations as the great day draws near; clothes, dealing with inquiries about wedding presents, correspondence over the invitations, and last but most important, the emotional strain of parting with her daughter.

THE MENU for the reception will have to be decided in good time. If a hotel or professional caterers are responsible, they will usually have one or two specimen menus to choose from, at varying prices.

WEDDING BREAKFAST. A typical menu for a Wedding Breakfast, i.e. a formal luncheon, would be:

Soup, or hors d'oeuvre, or smoked salmon or melon
Roast chicken with peas and roast potatoes and a green salad
Fruit salad with ice cream and *petits fours*
The wedding cake

With a menu of this kind, a variety of wines can be served appropriate to the various courses, or more usually, a good "all purpose" wine to go with the whole meal, with champagne served along with the wedding cake when the toasts are drunk.

BUFFET LUNCHEON. For a buffet luncheon, a

variety of sweet and savoury dishes, to be eaten with the fingers alone or with a fork, can be served. They can include sandwiches, bread rolls, canapés, patties, sausage rolls, sausages on sticks, small portions of salad, small cutlets or portions of cold meat or pie; sweet cakes and biscuits, individual fruit flans or fruit salad with cream, meringues, and pastries. Since most people find it difficult to manage a glass *and* a plate of food while standing up there must either be small tables for them to sit at, or alternatively, drinks may be circulated first (cocktails, sherry, or glasses of wine) and people can dispose of these before starting to eat, though usually one or two waiters would be circulating with trays of drinks while the food is being consumed, in case anyone wants a drink as well. Then, when the wedding cake is cut, a glass of champagne is brought to everyone to drink the toasts.

AFTERNOON RECEPTION. For an afternoon reception, the menu might be: bread rolls, small savoury sandwiches, canapés, small cakes and biscuits, tea, coffee, cocktails and soft drinks. Cocktails, sherry, or champagne or other wine can be served throughout or champagne simply produced for the drinking of the toasts.

If the bride's mother is herself planning to cater for the reception, with the help either of friends or a paid staff, the following is an approximate guide to the quantities that will be required for a buffet for 20 people:

30 small bread rolls or sausage rolls
30 small savoury sandwiches
30 canapés or small individual vol au vents

40 small cakes or sweet biscuits
6 pints of tea or coffee. 1½ pints of milk if tea is served. 1½ lbs. sugar.
4 bottles of champagne or white wine if this is to be served for toasts only, 9 bottles if it is to be served throughout the reception.

If a more substantial buffet is required, i.e. if it is to take the place of a formal luncheon and not an afternoon tea, the following might be served in addition:

20 small individual plates of salad with ham, chicken mousse, cold cutlet, vol au vent, etc.
5 fruit flans, fruit salad and/or ice cream
3 bottles of sherry

These quantities are an approximate guide only: in particular, if many children are among the guests, the quantities of food allowed will need to be increased by half as much again. An ample supply of fruit squash will also be needed for the children.

WINES FOR THE RECEPTION. The bride's father will usually undertake responsibility for choosing and ordering these, whether the other catering is in the hands of his wife or of a professional firm. If he is unused to judging wines, he will be well advised to rely upon the advice of either his wine merchant or the hotel manager who is doing the reception.

A medium dry white wine is usually served at weddings with a buffet meal, as it goes best with all the varied types of food, from chicken to wedding cake, served on these occasions; but if a formal luncheon including red meat or game is served, then a red wine would go best with these courses.

Wines for the reception

Champagne is, of course, the traditional wine to have at weddings, but it is quite expensive; the fact that many people proclaim that they "don't really care for champagne" may well be due to the fact that one so often has to drink the relatively cheaper and inferior stuff at weddings. Unless one is prepared to pay for a reasonably good champagne (say about £8.00 a bottle), it may be more satisfactory—especially if one's guests are good judges of wine—to serve some other white wine which can be bought in a good quality more cheaply. Alternatively, one can serve the best quality to start with, and something less distinguished later, when the guests' palates have been rendered less discriminating by food and tobacco smoke. Or one can serve champagne only for the toasts, and other white wine for the rest of the reception. It is really for the host to decide.

In planning the wines, don't forget that if professional caterers are handling them, corkage will be charged upon each bottle, which can add quite considerably to the total cost.

If the reception is at an hotel, one should be charged only for the bottles actually opened, but if in a hall or private house, make sure to arrange that the wine is supplied on a sale-or-return basis. One can then order enough to have a reserve supply and avoid the nightmare of running out of drink. If the professional waiters are in charge of opening the bottles, be sure to have a word with the head waiter about how long the supply is expected to last, and instruct him that the reserve supply is not to be broached until the host has been approached for permission. This is not meanness, but simply necessary organisation.

As regards quantities to order, one bottle of wine will serve six people if it is only for toasts, but if wine is being served throughout the reception, glasses will need replenishing approximately every half-hour and the amount ordered should be increased accordingly. Allow, too, for one drink for each of the band, waiters, and other staff attending the reception.

MUSIC FOR THE RECEPTION. Soft, light background music adds a great deal to the atmosphere of a wedding reception; it is especially useful in "making things go" if the guests do not know one another well. A small string band is ideal, but a single pianist can do very well (remember to make sure there is a good piano available) or a hired stereo or taped background music is cheaper and very trouble-free.

Many electrical shops offer equipment and records for hire, or advise about where to get them; entertainment agencies can supply bands. Discuss in advance whether the music played is to be light classical numbers and Viennese waltzes, or current hits and "pop" numbers, or a mixture of both. Also, whether there will be dancing, in which case suitable music for this will have to be ordered. Remember to allow space for the band at the reception, or, if a stereo is being used, detail someone to attend to it when necessary (a younger brother or cousin is usually quite glad to help with this).

FLOWERS FOR THE RECEPTION. These should be planned at the same time as the flowers for the church, and should complement the colour scheme of the bride's and bridesmaid's dresses. If a buffet meal is being served, do not have flowers on the tables with the food; they only get in the way. It is better to have large vases in the corners of the room, or other strategic positions.

If guests will be sitting down, either at small tables or to a formal meal at long ones, some flowers can be placed on the tables, but they should be kept low enough for people to see over them.

The bridal bouquet is usually placed in front of the wedding cake, which will be in a dominating position either in the centre of the buffet, in front of the bride at a formal luncheon, or on a small table to itself at one end of the room.

THE WEDDING CAKE. Whether or not the reception is at a hotel which takes complete responsibility, the cake is almost always made to order by an outside firm specialising in these; or, if the family includes a really good cook, it can be home-made and even home-iced, though this last is a difficult job and sometimes arrangements can be made to have a home-made cake professionally iced.

Plenty of good recipes for wedding cake are available, e.g. in *Mrs. Beeton's Cookery and Household Management*, (which also gives directions for icing, assembling and decorating a 3-tier cake). A further advantage of making a cake at home is that it can be made as long as possible in advance, as this rich type of cake improves with keeping. On the other hand a cake made by a firm does have a reliable "professional touch". It should be ordered a month to six weeks in advance.

In planning the size of the cake, decide whether it is to serve for the reception only, or whether pieces are to be sent to friends and relations who did not attend the wedding; also whether the old and rather charming tradition of keeping the small top tier uncut to be used as a Christening cake for the first baby, is to be followed.

SEATING FOR A FORMAL WEDDING BREAKFAST. If there is to be a formal wedding breakfast or luncheon (the two terms mean the same, except that aperitifs are not served before a "wedding breakfast" but may be before a luncheon) it will be necessary to plan the seating and arrange place cards, even if it is only for a small family party of twenty or so; if there are more than about 50 guests, it is advisable to have a seating plan drawn, to be on show in the anteroom where guests assemble before the meal, so that everyone can find where to go.

The usual arrangement of the seating is that the bride and bridegroom sit in the places of honour, either together at the head of the table if one long table is used, or together in the middle of one long side with the wedding cake directly in front of them in the middle of the table; or, if more than one long table is being used, together in the middle of one side of the top table, facing the rest of the guests and with the wedding cake in front of them.

The bride sits on the left of the groom with her father on her left and on his other side the bridegroom's mother, then ushers and bridesmaids alternately. Next to the bridegroom on his right sits the bride's mother, and next to her the father of the groom with the chief bridesmaid on his right, then the best man, other bridesmaids and ushers alternately. Other senior members of the two families,

Seating for wedding breakfast

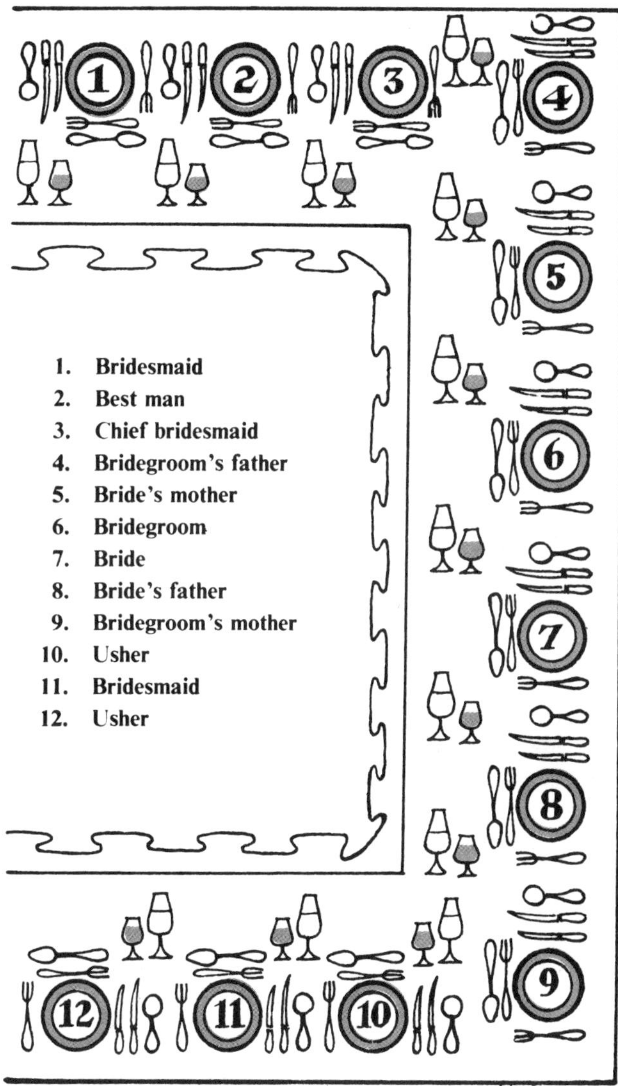

and any other specially honoured guests sit at the top table also. If preferred, the bridesmaids (other than the chief bridesmaid), ushers, best man and younger members of the two families may be placed here and there among the other guests, where they can help to look after people and generally see that everyone is enjoying themselves.

Arranging the place cards in accordance with the seating plan after the tables are laid, is a job that the bride's mother should delegate to a really reliable friend or relative.

If a buffet luncheon or afternoon tea is being served, with the guests at small tables, place cards and a formal order are not necessary; people just seat themselves in small groups as they like. But one or two tables, or one long table, at the top of the room, should be reserved for the immediate families, and any specially distinguished guests, and the bride's mother will show these people where to sit.

TRANSPORT TO THE RECEPTION. Guests at a wedding make their own arrangements for transport from the church to the reception; if it is not far and the weather is good, many will enjoy the walk and fresh air after the emotion of the church ceremony. Some who have cars will offer lifts to those who have not. The only people who need be provided with motor transport are the bride and groom, their parents, the bridesmaids, and any friends or relations who are actually staying at the home of the bride's parents for this occasion. It is, additionally, a courtesy to see that any elderly guests are offered a seat in a car, either one of the hired wedding cars or in one belonging to another guest.

Transport to the reception

For a country wedding, where guests will be arriving by train at a station which may be rather far from the church, the bride's father usually arranges for one or two cars to meet the appropriate trains and take guests to the church. But even this is not obligatory. For getting back to the station afterwards, there will usually be enough people with cars among the guests who will offer lifts to those who have to catch the train.

It is not always necessary to hire cars; it can often be arranged that the family cars are driven by hired chauffeurs for the day.

Any hiring arrangements should be made well in advance.

14

The Reception — on the day

The bride's parents and the parents of the groom are usually the first to arrive at the reception-place after the happy couple, but there is not time for prolonged greetings or talk because guests will be arriving almost at once.

The guests usually deposit any outdoor coats they don't wish to keep with them, in the cloakrooms, before proceeding to the reception room to be welcomed by the bride's mother and father (in that order) standing just inside the door. They should not indulge in prolonged conversation at this stage as it holds up the receiving line; there will usually be opportunities for further talk later on; only a brief remark or compliment is necessary now. If guests are not being announced by name on arrival, friends of the groom will probably need to introduce themselves by name to the bride's parents at this first greeting. The parents of the bridegroom stand next in the line and are greeted next, again only briefly. The bride and groom stand together a little farther on, either about ten feet away or, if preferred, at the far end of the room, and guests move on to speak to them and be introduced to whichever of the couple they don't already know. Here again, prolonged conversation at this stage will only hold up other guests.

At the well-organised reception, ushers, bridesmaids and other young members of the two families will be in readiness to take guests under their wing after passing the receiving line, and the two immediate essentials for these young unofficial hosts and hostesses are firstly, to see that everyone has a drink, and secondly, to chat pleasantly to anyone who seems not to know many people and to perform introductions and generally to see that nobody is out of things.

If there is to be a formal sitting-down to lunch or refreshments, the bride's mother will give the signal for this soon after the last of the guests has arrived. If a move is to be made to another room for the meal, the bride and groom usually go first, followed by the bride's father leading the bridegroom's mother, any other specially honoured or elderly guests, the best man and chief bridesmaid, then all the other guests in any order, and finally the bride's mother and the father of the groom.

The clergyman who performed the marriage ceremony, if he is present, is usually asked to say grace, after which the meal is eaten. It is not practical to have grace said unless people are sitting down to the meal all at one time.

A formal meal will be served by waiters in the usual way, but if it is a buffet meal it can either be served by waiters or the gentlemen can wait upon the ladies. If light refreshments only are being served, the waiters or waitresses usually stand behind the buffet on which the food is displayed, ready to help guests, or guests can just help themselves.

If champagne is being kept only for the toasts, it is served, along with the wedding cake, at the end of the meal, and all the toasts drunk then. But if wine is being served throughout the proceedings, then it is quite possible to start on the toasts earlier on, before the cake is cut.

TOASTS. At a very small and informal reception, the only toast may be that of the bride and bridegroom, but if there are more than a handful of guests, it is usual to have several toasts. Each person who replies to a toast, proposes the next one at the conclusion of his speech.

The most usual toasts are in this order:

"The bride and bridegroom"

Usually proposed by some old family friend who can be relied upon not to be too pompous or sentimental.

"The bridesmaids"

Proposed by the bridegroom at the end of his speech of thanks in reply to the first toast, in the course of which he also thanks the guests for their presents and the parents for giving the reception.

"The parents of bride and bridegroom"

Proposed by the Best Man at the conclusion of his speech of thanks on behalf of the bridesmaids. He ends with a special word of thanks to the parents of the bride as hosts on this occasion, and proposes the health of all four parents.

The bride's father usually makes a brief reply to this last toast and simply thanks everyone for their good wishes and says how pleased he is to see them and how much he hopes they are all enjoying themselves.

SUGGESTED SPEECHES

Proposing the health of the happy couple

"Ladies and Gentlemen, we are all here today to start Bill and Elizabeth out on their new life accompanied by our very best wishes, and it falls to my lot to propose the toast which is so near to all our hearts. I'm sure we all wish Bill and Elizabeth all the happiness in the world, now and always, and that they may be blessed with good health, enough wealth, and long life together.

It gives me very special pleasurc to propose this toast, because I have known Elizabeth almost all her life. I remember that she used to play with my own children, and how amused we all were with the pantomimes they put on at Christmas—Elizabeth was always most entertaining and displayed a fine sense of humour which I think is one of the most important ingredients for a successful marriage.

Bill I have not known quite so long, but I think we all feel happy that he and Elizabeth have chosen one another, and certainly Bill is a young man of great discernment and good sense—look at the girl he has chosen!

So, ladies and gentlemen, let us all join together in wishing them every happiness. I give you the toast of Bill and Elizabeth—God bless them."

The Bridegroom's Reply

This comes after the health of himself and his wife has been duly drunk. It is traditional for him to begin his speech with the words "My wife and I"—a signal for general laughter all round.

"Ladies and gentlemen, my wife and I would

like to thank you very much for the good wishes you have just expressed. To have you all here with us today has added enormously to the happiness of the most wonderful day in our lives, and one which we shall long remember.

I should like to take this opportunity of thanking Elizabeth's parents for giving us this lovely reception, which we are all enjoying so much, and for all the great kindness they have shown to me all along. I hope that our home will always be the happy and friendly place that their home has been to me.

Thank you all, too, for the quite wonderful gifts you have sent for our new home. We really feel exceptionally well set up! My wife asks me to say that we do hope you will all come and see us there very soon.

Finally, I must thank my friends who have acted as ushers, and the very charming bridesmaids who have been such a help to my wife and made such a bevy of beauty around her today. Ladies and gentlemen, will you join me in drinking the toast of The Bridesmaids?"

The Best Man's Speech

Since ladies do not, by tradition, speak at weddings, the best man replies on behalf of the bridesmaids. His speech should be along the following lines:

"Ladies and Gentlemen, it is one of the happiest of my duties today to thank you, on behalf of the bridesmaids, for your good wishes. I know it has been a great pleasure to them, and to all of us, to act as attendants at the marriage of Elizabeth and Bill. We should all like to reiterate the thanks which the bridegroom has already expressed to Mr. and Mrs. Jenkins who have been our hosts today. May I ask you to join with me in drinking the toast of the parents of the bride and groom?"

The Bride's Father's Speech

"Thank you all very much for your good wishes to my wife and myself, to Mr. and Mrs Brown" (the groom's parents) "and to our daughter and her husband. It has made my wife and me very happy to know that Elizabeth is starting her new life as a married woman in such auspicious circumstances and surrounded by the love and good wishes of so many friends. Perhaps one of the nicest things about a wedding is that it does make such a wonderful excuse for bringing together such a host of old friends. It has certainly been a great pleasure to see you all here today. Bill and Elizabeth will be leaving shortly as they have to get to the airport on time, but I do hope the rest of you will stay on and enjoy yourselves."

(This last remark should be taken with a pinch of salt; it is polite for a host to express such sentiments, but guests usually leave the reception quite soon after the bride and groom have departed.)

Needless to say, the speeches outlined above are intended as suggestions only. Other comments, anecdotes and compliments will probably suggest themselves in individual cases, and where they do so spontaneously, it is much better to adopt them, as they sound more natural than a set speech. There is no need to strain after humour in these speeches, however; where one can be witty and amusing naturally, by all means do so, but for those who have not this gift, a simple sincerity is best in speeches of this kind.

Following the speeches, the best man sometimes reads out the telegrams that have been received, but this can be rather tedious as usually the senders are unknown to most of those present and their messages are full of well-intentioned clichés; so a better plan is to have the telegrams either passed around or displayed so that those interested can read them.

CUTTING THE CAKE. The wedding cake, whether cut and handed round prior to the toasts or later in the proceedings, is always first cut by the bride, using her husband's sword if he is an officer. (As it isn't easy to cut a cake with a sword, have an incision made beforehand at a marked place, to be covered with only a thin top coat of icing.)

The bride makes the first cut only, after which the cake is cut up by the waiters and distributed either by them or—a rather more attractive custom —by the bridesmaids.

If there is dancing, it can begin immediately after the toasts. The bride and bridegroom open the dancing by making a few turns round the room together, after which others can join in.

Whatever form the reception takes, whether there is a wedding breakfast or not, dancing or not, the ideal thing is for the bride and groom to circulate among the guests and have a few minutes of conversation with everyone there; if there are many people there, they may have to split up in order to get round to everyone, but if time allows, they can go round together. If there is a formal meal and time is short afterwards, it may not be possible for them to speak to everyone, but it is nicer if they can.

GOING AWAY. When the time comes for them to go away to change for their honeymoon journey, the groom has the help of his best man, the bride of her bridesmaids.

The custom of the bride turning as she leaves the reception and throwing back her bouquet —preferably from a turn in the staircase—is a rather charming American tradition that is not very widely adopted here as yet; probably because English brides usually slip quietly away from the reception without any fuss, when they go to change. If, however, her going is noticed, or she feels she would like to adopt the idea of throwing back her bouquet (with the superstition that the girl who catches it will be the next bride) there is no reason why she shouldn't do so.

The bride's and groom's cases should already be packed for their journey and either stowed in the car that will take them away from the reception or, if a hired car is being used, at least all ready to be put in it, a job which the best man usually sees to. The best man and the chief bridesmaid also see to the tidying up and removing of the couple's wedding clothes, the return of the groom's morning dress if this has been hired, the packing away of the bride's white dress and veil in tissue paper and taking it to her mother's home to await her return from the honeymoon.

While the bride is changing, the bride's mother

goes to say goodbye to her daughter privately, as a proper farewell will hardly be possible at the actual moment of departure.

The bride and groom usually meet after changing and return to the reception room together to make a quick round of goodbyes to their nearest friends and relations; they will not be able to say an individual goodbye if there are more than about twenty guests, nor is it necessary.

While they have been away there will probably have been a certain amount of skylarking with the car in which they are to depart—old shoes tied on, at the very least, and "just married' chalked on the back. It is up to the best man to circumvent the more embarrassing manifestations of high spirits, to see that no odd packets of confetti find their way into the suitcases, and so forth. Still, these jokes have a genuine *raison d'être*—they help to tide over the inevitably difficult and emotional moment when the couple drive off into their new life.

AFTER THE RECEPTION. After the bride and groom have gone, the wedding reception usually breaks up quite quickly. It is not polite to leave before the bride, unless for some special reason which has been mentioned to the hostess previously, but now guests stay and chat just long enough to help the bride's parents get over the moment of parting with their daughter, then take their leave. Occasionally, if the wedding presents have not been on show at the reception, some of the closer friends may be invited back for a cup of tea and to view the presents at the home of the bride's parents, but this is by no means always done.

Sometimes, too, there is a festive evening organised for the immediate bridal party. The two sets of parents, with the brothers and sisters of the bride and groom, the ushers and best man and the bridesmaids, may go out to dine or dance, or may make up a theatre party. This again is by no means always done, but is a pleasant way to round off the day, which might otherwise end in anti-climax. Sometimes the bridegroom's father is host at these evening festivities, sometimes it is the father of the bride.

Two other formalities remain when the wedding is over. One is the sending of wedding cake to friends and relations who could not come to the wedding. Strictly speaking this is the job of the bridesmaids, working from a list compiled by the bride's mother; but it can equally well be done by the mother and sisters of the bride, or anyone else in the family circle.

Everyone who sent a present ought to be sent a piece of cake, whether they were invited to the wedding or not.

Alternatively, formal notices of the marriage, engraved or printed in black or silver upon a white card, are sent out to relations, friends and acquaintances who could not be at the ceremony—including, usually, quite a number who were not invited simply because the guest list had to be limited somehow. They can be sent to business acquaintances as well as personal friends.

The wording of such an announcement is as follows:

After the reception

Mr. and Mrs. Reginald Jones
have the honour to announce
the marriage of their daughter
Kathleen
with
Mr. George Smith
at
St. John's Church, Leyden Bush
on
Tuesday, 20th February, 1979.

No acknowledgement or return gift is necessary in the case of an announcement.

The second after-the-wedding formality, is that the bride should, if at all possible, invite everyone who was invited to the wedding, to visit herself and her husband in her new home. Obviously this is not always possible, especially if the couple are going away to live, but the general idea should be observed. If the bride is returning to live near her home district, she can give an "At Home" to include most of those who were at her wedding; or she can invite them individually to lunch, dinner, or tea, or just to drop in for a drink or for coffee. But something of this kind she should certainly do, if at all possible. It is the best of all ways of ensuring that her new life, like her wedding day, will be filled with affection, kindness and courtesy.

15

Photographs and Publicity

Some of the guests will almost certainly want to take photos both at the church and at the reception in these days when so many people are keen amateur photographers; but even so, if a really good photographic souvenir of the great day is wanted, it is best to call in a professional photographer as well. This should be arranged at least two weeks in advance. Sometimes the photographer will agree to come for a small fee if he has the chance of selling prints to the guests at the reception—in which case proofs will usually be rushed back to be on show before the reception is over. If he is selling only to the bride's family and not to guests, the fee is likely to be more—probably at least £100 and a small *pro rata* sum for finished prints ordered.

At least three groupings are usually taken after the wedding: the bride and groom; bride and groom with bridesmaids; and bride and groom with best man, bridesmaids and all the members of both their families. Other groupings can be arranged if desired. One of the nicest souvenirs is to have a photograph of the bridal party and all the guests if the number is not too great.

If the bride's photograph is being taken alone, it is best to have this done after she is dressed for the wedding and before setting out for the church.

In this case she will need to allow at least half an hour for photographs, and make sure the photographer is on hand in good time.

If the bride and groom have any local "news value", the local papers should be notified of the date of the wedding and asked if they wish to send a reporter and/or photographer. If either of the families is of social standing, this can be done with national papers also. It is best to get in touch with the newspaper several days in advance of the occasion, both because local papers usually publish only once a week, and in order to enable the news editor to plan his reporters' and photographers' visits in advance. The News Editor is the person to contact on a local paper, the Social Editor if the paper is a national daily.

REPORTS OF THE WEDDING. Most local newspapers prefer the account of the wedding to be sent in to them already written up; for one thing, this saves their reporters' time, and for another, it should ensure complete accuracy. Some papers like to send the bride's mother a form to fill in, with spaces for the names of the bride and groom, description of the clothes, etc. Failing that, a brief account along the following lines might be sent in:

> The wedding took place at St. Paul's Church on May 30, between Mr. James Dukes, youngest son of Mr. and Mrs. Charles Stuart Dukes, of Virginia Water, Surrey, and Miss Judith Mayweather, daughter of Mr. and Mrs. Malcolm Mayweather of The Lodge, Woking.

The Vicar, the Rev. Wilfred Chase, officiated. Given away by her father, the bride wore a dress of white brocade and a short tulle veil held in place by one large white rose. She carried a bouquet of white roses.

The bridesmaids were Miss Ann Mayweather (sister of the bride), Miss Jane Oliver and Miss Prudence Oliver, and there was one child attendant, Amanda Mayweather, niece of the bride; they wore dresses of pastel organdie with head-dresses to match, and carried posies of roses. Mr. Stephen Dukes, brother of the bridegroom, was best man, and a reception was held at the house of the bride's parents, after which the bride and bridegroom left for their honeymoon, which is being spent in Italy.

About fifty presents were received, including a refectory table and a set of Wedgwood china.

Remember that most local papers like to include as many people's names as possible in the report. If space is short that week, the report may be cut, but otherwise, it will probably be printed in full.

If the notice of the marriage is to appear in the "Births, Marriages and Deaths" columns of the paper, as distinct from the news column, it will have to be paid for. The cost for a national paper is about £40.00; less for a local paper. It should be worded quite briefly, as follows:

Dukes—Mayweather.—On Tuesday, 30th May at St. John's Church, James, son of Mr. and Mrs. Charles Dukes of Virginia Water, Surrey and Judith, daughter of Mr. and Mrs. Malcolm Mayweather, of The Lodge, Woking.

16

Memoranda

FOR THE BRIDE: Choose bridesmaids. With bridegroom, interview the clergyman who will perform the ceremony. Plan clothes for self, and for bridesmaids in consultation with them. Book hairdressing appointments well in advance. Compile a list of wedding presents wanted. Acknowledge all gifts promptly. See to new passport if necessary. Decide on music for the ceremony.

FOR THE BRIDE'S MOTHER: Newspaper announcement of engagement, and letters of announcement to friends. Interview hotel and/or caterers for reception and see to hire of hall, etc. Printing of invitations, printed service leaflets, and printed announcements of the wedding. Send out invitations. Order cake. With husband, order wines. Order photos. Interview florists about decorations for church and reception. Send invitations to people who will be house guests for the wedding. Deal with inquiries about wedding presents. Order small boxes for sending off pieces of cake. Talk husband into ordering his morning dress, and order a buttonhole for him. Plan own ensemble and book hair appointment. See to hire of waiters, music, glass and china, cutlery and table linen for the reception if not in a hotel. Do seating plan and place cards if a formal luncheon at the reception. Make a list of the guests for ushers. Decide whether wedding rehearsal necessary. Decide and arrange about the display of presents. Arrange about awning and carpet for church if wanted. Hire of cars in consultation with husband. Marriage announcements for insertion in newspaper. See that those who will be making speeches are warned what is expected of them. See about changing rooms for the bride and bridegroom. Send notice of marriage to newspaper.

FOR THE BRIDEGROOM: Interview with bride's father. Buy the engagement ring. With fiancée, interview clergyman and arrange about music, choir, type of ceremony, bell-ringing, etc. Choose best man and ushers. Buy wedding ring. Order morning dress. With fiancée, choose presents for bridesmaids. Order flowers for bride, bridesmaids, and the two mothers, in consultation with fiancée. Obtain licence or registrar's certificate if these are needed. Make arrangements, buy tickets, etc., for the honeymoon. Let other men of the immediate wedding party know if they are to wear morning dress. Order car to go to church and leave the church afterwards. Arrange a small bachelor dinner or informal party for the ushers. Reply to toast of The Bride and Bridegroom, and propose toast of The Bridesmaids.

BEST MAN: Order morning dress. Look after the ring and clergy fees, and the wedding journey tickets, etc. Have spare ring ready in case of emergency. Organise cars getting away from the church. Put luggage into car for honeymoon journey. Reply to toast of The Bridesmaids, and propose the toast of "The Four Parents". See to return of own and bridegroom's morning dress after the wedding day.

BRIDESMAIDS: See to own clothes in consultation with bride. Help bride to dress, help her with veil, hair, gloves, etc., both in getting ready, at the ceremony, and at the reception. Take round cake at the reception. Help bride to change her clothes afterwards, and make arrangements for the wedding dress to be looked after till her return. Help to send off slices of cake after the wedding.

BRIDE'S FATHER: Check transport arrangements. Order morning dress and buttonhole. See to wines. Reply to toast of the parents. Try to keep wife and daughter calm—and be prepared to write enormous cheques!

17

The Wedding Budget

It must be emphasized that the costs of a wedding, as given in the following pages, are estimated only approximately. With every item listed, it would perhaps be possible to spend less, by careful management and cutting costs. It would be equally possible—and indeed, easy—to exceed the estimated costs by a considerable sum, if one is not worried by the need for economy and can afford to think only of the total effect. The figures offered here are intended only as a guide in planning the wedding, so that those responsible can work out the plans for the ceremony and reception, with a full knowledge of the scale of expenditure that may be involved.

The Bridegroom's Expenses

Engagement and wedding rings	from £100.00
Marriage Licence or Fee for Registration Certificate	variable
Marriage certificate	variable
Hire of car to church, and from church to reception,	from £80.00
from reception to station or airport	variable
Flowers for bride, bridesmaids, mothers, and ushers	from £80.00
Hire of morning dress, etc.	from £35.00

The wedding budget

Bridesmaid's presents	from £15.00
Fee to clergyman	variable
Fee to clerk	variable
Fee to Parochial Church Council	variable
Fee for church (if any)	variable
Organ and choir	variable
Bells	variable
Tip to verger	from £5.00
Honeymoon expenses	variable

Expenses of the Bride's Father

Bride's outfit	from £100
Cost of buffet reception for 100 guests	from £400
or	
Cost of wedding breakfast for 100	from £450
Wine for 100	from £225
Wedding cake	from £40.00
Champagne for 100 for toasts	from £150
Tips	from £30.00
Flowers for church and reception	from £40.00
Car hire	variable
Invitations and order of service leaflets	from £75.00
Postage for invitations	from £15.00
Newspaper announcements in national paper—engagement	from £40.00
marriage	from £40.00
Photos	from £100
Hire of morning dress	from £35.00
Music for reception	variable

MANNERS MAKETH MARRIAGE. Every bride rightly wants her wedding day to be something to be remembered with happiness by all those present. It is for this reason that etiquette is important at a wedding: it helps to prevent those small difficulties, hurt feelings, unintentional slights and other minor unpleasantnesses which might spoil things for any individual.

But it should never be forgotten that good manners are important not only on the wedding day itself but throughout the married life of the couple. A husband and wife will naturally relax at home, in the company of one another; but they should never allow this relaxation to go so far as to do away with the courtesy that is due from each to the other.

Minor sins against good manners, such as interrupting one another's remarks when in company, or making would-be comical or satiric comments on one's partner to an outsider, or being less punctual for a date with one's husband than one would be with anyone else, or making witty disparaging remarks about one's wife's driving, are most unattractive and are unfortunately easy to fall into. A good deal of self-discipline is one remedy, but the right attitude of mind toward one's marriage partner is even better.

This does not mean that they must keep up a pretence to one another. Obviously the modern husband is going to see his wife in a facepack or night cream at some time, the wife will see her husband untidy and unshaven. This does not preclude the exercise of good manners—one can show kindness and consideration just as well when one is untidy as when dressed for an evening out.

Manners maketh marriage

There will be plenty of ways in which both partners can make it plain that they respect each other, and value the other as a person who comes first in their thoughts.

Every happily married couple knows that courtesy can flourish under the most unexpected conditions, and that it is the outward small-change of their underlying regard.

If their home is to be the friendly, happy place that most couples want it to be, courtesy towards outsiders becomes important too. The newlyweds should not become so totally wrapped up in one another that they neglect the normal conventions and usages of ordinary society. Meetings with friends, contacts with neighbours, entertaining (formal or otherwise), all these have an important role in bringing the new household into a good relationship with the rest of the community.

And later on, when there are children, their upbringing becomes so much easier if good manners, gentle speech and habitual courtesy is the rule of the home. Then they will not have to be taught these things, but will absorb them imperceptibly from earliest youth.

In marriage and family life, just as in other human relationships, courtesy is no substitute for a good heart and right thinking; rather it is the everyday expression of these good qualities, something without which life would be a great deal the poorer.

Index

Index

Index

Index